Letters of Transmission

Alfred R. Pulyan, self-portrait

Letters of Transmission

*The Enlightenment Method
of Zen Master Alfred Pulyan*

Edited by
Bart Marshall

REALFACE PRESS

Published by Realface Press
info@realface.com

© Bart Marshall 2019
First Edition 2019

ISBN: 978-0-9862035-5-8

Cover art: "Alfred Pulyan," by Richard Stalter
Courtesy of Nicholas Gallucci collection

Regarding the question of death:
The body dies and is dissipated.
The mind is one with the body at all times
and is therefore also dissipated.
Nothing of <u>you</u> remains.

— Alfred Pulyan

<u>Also published by Realface Press:</u>

Christ Sutras*: The Complete Sayings of Jesus
from All Sources Arranged into Sermons,*
compiled and composed by Bart Marshall

The Perennial Way*, Extended Edition,*
translated by Bart Marshall

Bhagavad Gita*: The Definitive Translation,*
translated by Bart Marshall

The Triune Self*: Confessions of a Ruthless Seer,*
by Mike Snider

The Conquest of Illusion, by J.J. van der Leeuw,
90th Anniversary Edition, edited by Bart Marshall

After the Absolute, by David Gold with Bart Marshall

Think and Grow Rich, by Napoleon Hill,
80th Anniversary Edition, edited by Bart Marshall

Magic, White and Black, by Franz Hartmann, M.D.,
edited by Bart Marshall

The Torah*: The Five Books of Moses,
King James Readers' Version,* by Bart Marshall

Verses Regarding True Nature, by Bart Marshall

Pearl of the Orient, a screenplay by Bart Marshall

Introduction

You hold in your hand a unique treasure. There have been thousands of spiritual teachers, but true masters — those who can *transmit*, who can midwife a student to awakening — are rare. Some of them may write books or essays, but their real work is done individually with students in person.

Alfred Pulyan (1896-1966) was considered an American Zen master, but not Zen in the formal Japanese tradition. Rather, Zen in the sense of going directly to the heart of the matter without regard for scriptures or traditions. Pulyan was one of those rare spiritual masters who could transmit to others, and his method of transmission came not only through personal contact, but through an exchange of letters with his students. In fact, he worked primarily by mail and had notable success triggering enlightenment in serious students through the confrontation and rapport of his letters.

A fortunate side-effect of his method is that it is written down, and thus potentially available to others — providing one can find any of his letters. Those collected here are from correspondence with Richard Rose in 1960 and 1961, and provide an invaluable look under the covers as a Zen master goes about his thankless work.

Rose was already awake when he heard about Pulyan's ability, having had a conclusive spiritual experience in 1947 at age thirty. He found out about Pulyan in a conversation with a man who impressed Rose with his sincerity and dedication to spiritual seeking. Rose asked him if he'd found any books or teachers of particular value in his search. The man said, "Yes, one book, *The Conquest of Illusion*, and one teacher, Alfred Pulyan, who can transmit, and who works primarily through the mail."

Rose was intrigued and contacted Pulyan for the purpose of learning how to transmit what he'd become, pretending to be a seeker while continually pressing Pulyan to reveal method. At times in these letters Pulyan seems to be onto him, but with unbelievable patience and mastery he works to crack Rose's nut while at the same time telling him what he's doing and how and why he's doing it.

Pulyan wrote his letters in longhand, with extensive margin notes. For this book, I have edited them to include those notes in the main text, and made other minor edits to help the letters read more smoothly. Rose's letters are not included in this book, except for his initial inquiry that kicks things off.

Not much is known about Pulyan's life, and in fact he's somewhat of an enigma. Much of what is known he tells us himself in these letters. Conflicting reports have him being born either in New York or London, but at any rate he turned up in New York City sometime after World War I and lived most of his life there. He is of an age where he might have served in the war, but no record of it exists. From these letters we know he studied mathematics and worked as an accountant, office manager, and executive.

In the late 1950's he and his wife Madeline bought twelve acres in rural Connecticut with money Pulyan received in a settlement after being hit by a truck or bus in New York. They settled in there, and some close spiritual friends also lived on or near the property. One of these friends was Ruthie Lennon, who was Pulyan's teacher, and who was instrumental in his realization. He writes of her: "One day while investigating a new psychotherapy I met a very self-possessed young lady, married, cheerful. I spoke to her, and then tried all my intellectual equipment—the philosophers, scientists and so forth. She handled these very easily. Compared to me she was deep water, deeper than my sonic apparatus could register. Could she be deeper than Vedanta, Shin-shu, Taoism, Zen? I was incredulous, but it has worked out."

We have these valuable letters because Rose kept all his correspondence over his many years as a spiritual teacher, and because his students have transcribed and preserved them. In addition to his published books, Rose also left mountains of unpublished writings, many of which have been transcribed and made available on websites by his students.

Of particular note in this regard is tatfoundation.org, which is the official site for the TAT Foundation, which Rose founded, and which holds four gatherings a year. Other notable websites with Rose's writings, as well as other valuable spiritual writings, include searchwithin.org, selfdefinition.org, selfdiscoveryportal.com, and albigen.com.

Pulyan's only known published writings are articles in *The Aberree,* a journal in circulation from 1954 through 1965. The best known of these, "The Penny That Blots Out the Sun," is included at the end of this book.

1074 High St
Benwood, W. Va.
August 17, 1960

Mr. Alfred R. Pulyan

I have your address from Mr. McIntyre of Santana California.
I consider Mac to be very conservative about recommending
anyone to subscribe to anyone or anything....so I feel that
I may have much to gain from writing to you.

I like to tell people that I am a seeker after Truth, or the
Truth. I have been pretending thus for several decades, being
43,, but as yet I do not know what the Truth is so cannot even
say that I know that for which I am seeking. I have explored
many religions and cults,-and a couple secret organizations.
Am still riding the horns of the dilemma that follows trying
to weigh one against another.

Mac says that you pursue expansion of consciousness. Although
I have come to look upon reason as the vanity of the intellect
(mind) still when it comes to checking a movement to see if I
want to put my entire life's energy into the quest,--I find
myself using or trying to use reason to qualify it.

I will be glad to correspond with you if you think it no great
waste of time for you, and will furnish any information
about myself that you wish. Also request at this point that
you brief me a bit on what you are about. Mac was not specific
and since I know that he looked into many movements,   do not
know too much except that he places you in a position that is
of benefit to sincere students of the Truth.

I am enclosing an envelope to expedite reply.

Richard Rose

4

August 17, 1960

Mr. Alfred E. Pulyan,

I have your address from Mr. McIntyre, of Santana, California. I consider Mac to be very conservative about recommending anyone to subscribe to or anything...so I feel that I may have much to gain from writing you.

I like to tell people that I am a seeker after Truth, or The Truth. I have been pretending thus for several decades, being 43, but as yet I do not know what the Truth is so cannot even say that I know that for which I am seeking. I have explored many religions and cults, and a couple secret organizations. Am still riding the horns of the dilemma that follows trying to weigh one against another.

Mac says that you pursue expansion of consciousness. Although I have come to look upon reason as the vanity of the intellect (mind), still when it comes to checking a movement to see if I want to put my entire life's energy into the quest, I find myself using or trying to use reason to qualify it.

I will be glad to correspond with you if you think it no great waste of time for you, and will furnish any information about myself that you wish. Also request at this point that you brief me a bit on what you are about. Mac was not specific, and since I know that he looked into many movements, I do not know too much except that he places you in a position that is of benefit to sincere students of the Truth.

I am enclosing an envelope to expedite reply.

Sincerely,
Richard Rose

P.S. what is the answer.
I think it is this, the "good soil" or
hopeful student already knows the game
somewhat, by instinct. Others try to use
judgment & reason & get all conjangulated!

ALFRED R. PULYAN
R. F. D.
SOUTH KENT, CONN.

Sept-17, 1960.

Dear Richard,

It is necessary to establish some communication
between us, even if I have to wave a rattle to do it.
So come out from the corner & don't look at me that way!
("Joke" please note. I refer to our treatment of psychotics, humorously)
But one must have something in common - - -

I suppose the only thing is to look at the
positive statements you make & see what you DO say.
So! : —

ADVICE!!
(1) "It is up to you to validate "certain claims" or try another tack".

(a) "up to you" like a child saying "up to you mother to do this or that,
because you love me, or I shall throw myself in the river."
Actually you speak as though I wished to gain converts to a movement!
There is no "movement"!.
It is desirable that you should "validate" me, & actually essentially
part of the process, but I can force nothing & directly prove nothing.
Could Santama or Jesus? No - only words. Their disciples had to invent
a crop of "miracles" which actually help not at all in our great &
Santama & Jesus protested that several times. Cf Santama's story of
the ferryman & the monk who could walk on the water.

THERE IS NO
MIRACLE
HOWEVER
SPECTACULAR
TO CHANGE YOU.
EVEN GOD
CANNOT DO IT!
(OBVIOUSLY)

(b) "try another tack" Surely the "technique" is not your affair.
You are not that objective yet!. The usual agreement is that the
student agrees to continue whatever happens, or is said, & the Zen
monk is kept waiting a day or so before he even gets through the
gate. Your ego is RIDING HIGH still, & that just won't do,
because it is the reverse of our objective.

YOU MUST
GIVE ME THE
REINS. I AM
NOT FORCING
ANYTHING —
MERELY BEING
AVAILABLE.

(2) "I am interested in knowing the truth"

MILDLY
INTERESTED?

There is only one way & that is to quit the egocentric position.
This is rough & needs a catalyst, a friend, an outside fulcrum.
One must first "decide not to decide" which is IMPOSSIBLE -- so
one has to have help in dropping "decision itself, ... once ...
No push-button methods exist, Jesus you remember looked sadly at
one young man, God will not come for you with a wheelbarrow!
So face it! Either you get nowhere while you live or you do it
the hard way. No "royal" road !!!!! (made easy for kings & Richard Rose)
So. I ask HOW MUCH INTERESTED? Enough to do violence to

A typical letter from Pulyan

Dear Richard,

Mac is very kind, and your letter is very straightforward. As Mac may have told you, I am not a believer in polite phrases but feel that to save time we should tell the truth as best as we can. You are 43, no longer young, and in a position I found intolerable. Like you, I was a "seeker," but it is obvious no words will satisfy you. Otherwise let us publish them in the newspapers. From this, the vanity of using mind (intellect) in the search is obvious.

However, as you say, it is all we have, so at the same time as you recognize the vanity of the instrument you have to use it to consider, for example, what Alfred (this writer) is all about. It is all vague and tantalizing — not even to know what you are and what is to become of you.

Consider this from Alfred's standpoint, if you can. He tries to "work" only with likely cases. Even then success is not 100%. He gets months, even years, of misunderstanding and trouble from each one of these, and more gray hairs. They are not to blame. They are using a mind which is amazingly persnickety and easily slips into mere debating society argument on every minute point, so that the forest is lost in the trees. Not knowing the result aimed at, they are usually not deeply dedicated, and things go in one ear and out the other.

He cannot tell them that as far as he knows he is their only hope — and that an uncertain one — unless they wish to go somewhere for personal work, say to a Zen instructor or to Subud. He knows something that people call "God," and it governs his life. But it does not govern theirs. They can be flippant about it. He can not. One day they may say, "This is obvious," but until then they cannot believe, and every inch of the way is a hard fight.

He has to be tough with them to remove their obstacles, but they interpret it as quarreling—as though he would waste weary time in that form of amusement. This is written at 2:30 a.m., for example, and the weight of the 3,000,000,000 people in the world seems at such an hour very oppressive. Further, he knows that not one of them can be trusted or treated as a real friend until after their "awakening." They are treacherous, in fact, at some point. I wonder if Jesus had even one friend.

The world seems stranger to me, perhaps, than even to you. Perhaps I could find only one out of several tens of thousands who would understand this. Why not tell me as much as you can of your early upbringing and religion, and those things you have since studied and your opinion about them—indeed, open up about your real sentiments.

Cordially,
Alfred

Dear Richard,

You certainly don't sound like a fool and that is half the battle. As long as you realize that the "self" is like an eel dipped in oil. Your problem is the old koan: "What shall I do when I meet a Zen master?" Shall I give him an uppercut, biff him, plug him? Well, if you do, he will either give you a little Judo, if he is a black belt, or, if he is an old man and weak, will politely transfer you to another monastery. Shall I call him a liar? He will smile and I shall get no further. Besides, after knowing him some time I shall see that he is sincere.

Then there is the possibility that he is self-deceived, in a state of illusion, mental conjangulation, misunderstanding of subjective experiences. Who isn't? After knowing him a little longer I may find him keen, sharp, definite, logical, certainly not psychotic, and I begin to say, "Hell. God or no God, give me some of that anyway!"

But right now I have just met him. How shall I act? Shall I doubt and yet half hide it, placate him so that he won't run away? If there is a chance that he really is that extraordinary thing, a Buddha, another Jesus, a Lao Tse, an Eckhart, then let us not lose this chance! So let us cajole a bit, smarm a bit, flatter the old bastard, kiss his venerable posterior, hide our doubts. The trouble is that the Zen master knows that one too! Besides if he needs that he is no good, strictly for the birds. Try somewhere else.

Of course you could just be a friend, and friends don't have any communication problem. Be clear at the outset—we are equal. You are a run-of-the-mill intelligent man—no less than me, no more than me as regards capacity. As regards knowledge, we have both picked up scraps. My mind is not more or less "infinite" than yours. I am no "better" or "worse" than you. We are both mixtures.

Our communication is normal. I cannot, however, describe the transcendental aim of our "work." I may try to do so now and then—if so laugh at me! It cannot be done. It is not something "added" —you would not find me or my friends too exceptional. We get up, eat, work round the place, look at TV, discuss, and all that you do. But we do know what underlies the whole caboozle—and went through hell to get it!

Avoid the highly "advertised" persons. The awakened ones are usually unknown, and you may meet one without suspecting it in any way. We can have a "transcendental" thing right now—friendship and confidence. From that, it is but a step. But such things cannot be forced. They must be spontaneous, natural, real—like the taste of a glass of water.

As far as a "relative bicameral approach," leave that to me and just be yourself. And be truthful—remorselessly so. That will help me most. Don't cover up. If what we seek is the Truth and the Way of the Universe, it can stand honesty I hope! Remember always that I know the whole game and this is nothing new—not the first time by any means!

Am I an "incomprehensible man"? My wife doesn't seem to appreciate my "greatness"! She finds me very ordinary—as indeed I am. Yet that is personality only. I could well be one-in-a-million because I found what I was looking for (as can you) and that is rare—but to work by "mail" is even rarer. I do not know of many cases.

Where could you go? To your ridiculous "brotherhood"? Well, they have the right doctrine

(Wisdom Religion) many of them, but they don't take you to the experience—usually. That would scare away the paying clients.

Is "attacking" the method? Yes and no. If you call "attack" the necessary exposure of every ego trick, then it is sharp attack. I assure you it can not be pleasant for either of us. If you are smart enough to see that friends can say anything whilst steadily maintaining their relationship then something can be done. Every step is contra-ego and that is a synonym for disagreeable, isn't it? I got mad with my teacher. I got physically murderous. Ego doesn't relinquish its "boss" idea without mayhem, squawks, screams, evasions, smarming...

At times the student tries to discredit the master. At other times he withdraws. There is a black leopard on the stairs. You meet him! What will you do? You can't pretend he isn't there. You can run away, you can fight furiously, you can say "nice pussy," you can try tricks to divert him, you can call for help—you can try many things. But he must eat you.

You will never be attacked or abused without reason. In business it is understood that when you say, "You are a low-down crook," you are being friendly (if you smile), and merely mean, "You are asking too much but I have to have the goods."

God comes easiest if you tell him he has made a mess of things. Try it! He is so grateful that at least you acknowledged his existence that he comes through with seventh-heaven ecstasies.

Can you "defend"? Why not—if it is not debating society or sophist tactics. It must be genuine and strictly reasonable. There is no hope at all for the fuzzy-minded!

There is no "emotion" in this. Love is

"heightened awareness," not a variable emotion, and it can be hard. But always it is outgoing and thinks not of itself, only of the other person. Our aim is "heightened awareness." Our aim is a Consciousness you have certainly never known, and which is amazing.

Regarding the question, "What happens after death?" The body dies and is dissipated. The mind is one with the body at all times and is therefore also dissipated. Nothing of you remains.

There is no survival or reincarnation or "immortal soul," or "conscious entity." As far as that goes, you are the exact equal of a drop of water and have the same possibility! Or an electron. Or a cabbage. Grim? Not at all. This is the wonderful truth, and is the purpose of our work. The Zen master asks, "What happens to you when the great Universe disappears in fire?"

If you have had some inklings of experiences, even the transient ones, if you are discriminative and can balance (almost) imponderables, if you are cunning and smart with true self-interest (like a serpent), then there is a chance. But Jesus said "few."

I do not fool myself. We shall see if you lose yourself in mere back-and-forth stuff, or if you take your chance. God knows—and that is no platitude. Remember, however, that facts are facts, and "knowing" them makes no difference, except to your peace of mind. What will happen to both of us is the same whatever we say or do!

With fingers crossed, but always,

Friend,
Alfred

P.S. Don't mix things. Keep my letters

confidential to yourself—especially as regards Mac. Naturally, you are similar in many ways, but this is a one-one thing and won't work in consultation! In other words, to "avoid" awakening is quite easy. 3,000,000,000 do that. To attain it is something else. "Messiah-jumpers" just don't.

Dear Richard,

This won't do you know! What won't do? Well, this horsing about as to what I am, what I can do and so forth. "Your plans," "your system," and so on! If only we could get down to the absolute friendship I asked, then all this by-play might be avoided. That means plain speaking and not "easing into an acquaintanceship."

If you call me a lousy son-of-a-bitch, an authoritarian snob, a hopeless paranoiac, then fine, excellent. But the dribbling, hopeless, piddling dialectic you favor me with is far more objectionable. You may call it polite and think you are behaving admirably, but it is of no use in our task. I have something — all that man can get on this earth, most probably — and my job and yours is to transfer it from me to you. Here is Alfred, the guinea pig. How are we to extract it from him? It is called *transmission*.

Now, in order to get you out of this weary, dreary back-and-forth I naturally try to find your reaction and get you to express it. I also relate my experiences with others, and so forth — all so as to throw enough stuff so that you will get an inkling of the position.

I do not, of course, betray confidences or names, but I do speak generally. For example, today I got a letter from a man who says he began to "pierce the darkness" about a year ago, and says truth is in Zen, Buddhism, Theosophy, Rosicrucianism, Quabalah, etc., and wants to <u>teach me</u>. He says I doubt my own capabilities and no doubt I will never meet "a truly awakened one."

Question: Can I do anything here? We never

really know. To debase and debauch the wonder I know so well is impossible, yet I cannot say straight out to him, "I <u>am</u> one of these truly awakened ones," although I can imagine ways in which I could have more of what I have.

I have met quite a number of "truly awakened" ones, but never so advanced as my own teacher who lives near me and is as unknown as any of us. The Buddha, Gautama, missed much of the physical side, for example, and even Zen does not stress it—although the Zen masters I have met had splendidly flexible bodies and quick reflexes.

Any evidence of pride or superiority, of course, damns the person at once. The master's "authority" is <u>lent to him</u> by the student for a purpose—it is delegated. It is <u>not welcome</u> to the master, who earnestly hopes for the day the student will dig him in the ribs and they will converse arm in arm about other things. It is a surgeon's job, but more thankless.

Now as to this case. Your mention of occult societies is a warning signal. I have not met a person truly awakened by any of these, although numbers of people do get a sort of "mental" awakening, wherein they see the "oneness" of things. It is good, but it is the cake without the icing. They do not know the One—as you and I could know one another. Nothing less will do! Note my exact words. They are those of DeGama in 1540 and of Jesus in AD30—or indeed of any truly awakened person.

One of my correspondents says he is spending his life in search of "St. Germain"! He will sooner find…(invent your own simile). Another says he is an Adept of the Fifth Ray and Master of the Spheres. (And so compensates for a depressing life!) So I ask him who his teacher was, but have little hope here.

Then there is the maiden lady who believes everything can be done through deliberate ESP. Says she knows cases where people do it in business for a good living. Says mystical glimpses give people no right to be authorities. Etc. etc. The word "authority" is based on the idea of "learning" things, as in astronomy, engineering, etc., and the "mystical glimpses" is a tricky way of referring to satori—which is something quite otherwise!

The "glimpse" is feeling. Satori is knowledge and much more. ESP is a do-it-yourself technique, and in any case, is ego's way of bloating himself as big as an ox to try to be something. There is no hope of "getting there" by heightened perceptions or ESP. It must be by *awareness of awareness*, not awareness of thoughts and things.

It is a characteristic evasion, and under pressure she will try every trick in the book and a flood of dialectics. She wants a boy friend! (This is one of the "occupational hazards" of the therapist—if you can call our work a therapy, which it includes and resembles.)

Now comes a letter from somebody called Richard. Seems a nice enough fellow, crazy, anxious on the one hand not to frighten me away and on the other pretty blah, blah. Tells me, "I must know a lot more about you." My momentary feeling is, "Go f--- yourself. What do you expect for the price of a stamp?" Then I say, "Down, Fido! After all he is entitled to be a skeptic. You were one yourself, Alfred—and how!" I was a lulu all right—far more of a smart aleck than you, indeed poisonous. Yet my friend did the job. Glory, hallelujah! I really didn't deserve it. So why should I get proud? But it is an effort!

Wants to know what happens if body and

mind disappear? Answer: You will be dead, my bucko, as you will discover one day! (Why do they say such stoopid things?) Oh well, maybe he had better come and see me one day—not for "the work," but to see that body and mind are still around! Make an appointment first—and not yet awhile. Mail work is as good as personal work—probably better.

Evidently Richard is a bit on the occult or magical side. (What the hell do they expect—levitation?) The real magic, which is a complete reversal of everything, never occurs to these numskulls.

As for "we are equal," this may be false in one way. People vary in "accessibility." Some attain in 30 minutes. Others take years of backbreaking and heartbreaking work. But Richard wants to go to the "heart of things." He is probably going <u>nowhere</u>.

"Your <u>system</u>," he keeps saying. <u>Your</u> system! I sell nothing, and everything is spontaneous. In Zen it is not the koan, but another and more personal factor that does the trick. Meditation is a device to keep the boys out of mischief for awhile. It doesn't succeed nowadays. They set out and have big feasts and go after the chicks with the slanted eyes.

It is his whole life, his whole health and happiness, and the God-forsaken idiot is going to throw it away by ungenerous, piddling, unfriendly communications. I could be sad if it wasn't happening all the time. Evidently he doesn't trust his friend Mac (if he is a friend), and is of a grudging, constipated mentality incapable of much fine feeling or "greatness." Some seed fell on good ground, some on stony soil, some by the wayside.

What will happen here? Doubtful prospect. He could get there, but he is still going around "judging" and "deciding." Since the essence of our work is to abandon this final line of defense of the ego, where can the change occur? What do I (Alfred) matter? If I were Oral Roberts, Walt Disney or a bum hopping freights it is all the same. Our aim is not the "accidentals." We shall see.

Another case. A "Scientologist." He has a "spirit" that has lived for 74 trillion years and has 2 trillion to go—on the "average." (What average?) During this time he "plays games," and after that he gracefully flops into Infinite Mind (unless it sidesteps with a shudder). His "thetan" or spirit or "self" can detach itself from the body and live without it—or at least that is his "ideal." (He has not quite reached it yet.) Nor can he yet read books in distant libraries. (Not enough ESP?) He is "self-determined"— completely so. In fact, he is invulnerable and inaccessible—unless life teaches him a sad lesson. I have known Scientologists, however, who were more accessible. One wrote: "Now I see myself, silly, fatuous." But it is rare. All these things are modes of ego.

Now as regards yourself and your letter. You want a process that "enhances." What does that mean—gives you joy and pleasure? This will not! What do you want to know about me before you start "work"? How can you know? There is no "aim" and no "system."

From my side, however, I am undertaking a long and difficult job that will add to my gray hairs. I am taking a bright child almost, still green behind the ears, and trying to show something of deep—what shall I say—of the highest feelings, the highest culture, maybe? But all words are wrong of course. Anyway, your current cynicism and world weariness is of no use here. You must somehow pitch yourself pretty high before this comes to you. You may deceive or cajole me, but not God.

I shall expect you to answer promptly, and to do as you are told. Also to cut out other similar work entirely and not read any books on this general subject (unless I happen to suggest one). Also send me a stamped addressed envelope. It will be unpleasant, frustrating, disagreeable, annoying... (but so is growing up). Afterwards you will be a human being and understand many things. The alternative is something (an average life) that will seem normal to you no doubt, but which from my present point of view is unthinkable. Nevertheless, we can part in the most friendly manner and nothing has been lost.

Friend,
Alfred

P.S. "Personality," which derives its characteristic "flavor" from memory content (both mental and physical "memories" or "habits") — and which is therefore largely accidental — is not the part of you we have to work with, <u>nor the part of me that works with you</u>. However, we have to use words and we have to pass through the mind, of course.

Now the mind, like everything in this world of ours, is strictly bipolar, dual. An obvious doublet is good-bad. There are thousands upon thousands since the mind splits everything It is the way of reasoning, the yes-no method. Light-dark, few-many, up-down, long-short, being-nonbeing, something-nothing, wise-foolish...

Thus it is idle to hope to "improve" personality since the side we show implies the side we suppress. However we can decide not to put any more disgusting junk into our memory box. There is sufficient already.

Consciousness or awareness is <u>pure</u>, but mixed up with (normally) some thought or perception. Yoga tries to free it, but it is actually the ego trying to free the ego and it leads maybe to a "feeling" experience, but not to "knowledge." We must accept our dual nature, like the vine winding round the tree.

If the student gets caught in personality (nothing unusual in a world where it is happening all day long, where every word is weighed to see if it is a "slight" or an ego-bruise), then he will start (or try to start) an old-fashioned interminable argument: "You were being needlessly rude." "I didn't mean it the way you think." "I want to be helped up not knocked down." "You are a fine one to talk of ego, you have an interesting amount yourself." "I want to learn something, not to have everything questioned." "Can't we get together somehow?" "Communication is breaking down." On and on—almost connubial, but not so snide.

Actually this is all very silly, and is avoided even in business circles where "everything goes," if it is said with a smile. ("You old crook!") Ego is very sensitive to words, even a waiter saying, "Not that fork, sir." But when ego is really threatened, take cover—the place will be in shambles.

No wonder so few attain to "life," and so many use push-button or internal methods like magic, occultism, etc., where one deceives oneself as long as possible.

Alfred

Dear Richard,

It's necessary to establish <u>some</u> communication between us, even if I have to wave a rattle to do it. So come out from that corner and don't look at me that way! ("Joke," please note. I refer to our treatment of psychotics humorously.) But one must have something in common. I suppose the only thing is to look at the positive statements you make and see what you <u>do</u> say. So:

1. *"It is up to you to validate 'certain claims' or try another tack."*

(a) *"...up to you..."* This is like a child saying, "It's up to you, Mother, to do this or that because you love me — or I shall throw myself in the river." You speak as though I wished to gain converts to a movement! There is <u>no</u> "movement." It is desirable that you should "validate" me, and is an essential part of the process, but I can force nothing and directly prove nothing. Could Gautama or Jesus? No, only words. Their disciples had to invent a crop of "miracles," which actually help not at all in our quest, and Gautama and Jesus protested several times. (Gautama's story of the ferryman and the monk who could walk on the water.) There is no miracle, however spectacular, to change you. Even God cannot do it! (Obviously.)

(b) *"...or try another tack."* Surely the "technique" is not your affair. You are not that objective yet! The usual agreement is that the student agrees to continue — whatever happens or is said — and the Zen monk is kept waiting a day or so before he even gets through the gate. Your ego is riding high still, and that just won't do — because it is the reverse of our objective. You must give me the reins. I am not forcing anything, merely being available.

2. *"I am interested in knowing the truth."* Mildly interested? There is only one way, and that is to quit the egocentric position. This is rough, and needs a catalyst, a friend, an outside fulcrum. One must first "decide not to decide," which is impossible, so one has to have help in dropping "decision" itself—once. No push-button methods exist. Jesus, you remember, looked sadly at one young man, "God will not come for you with a wheelbarrow!" So face it. Either you get nowhere while you live, or you do it the hard way. There is no "royal road" made easy for kings and Richard! So I ask, "How much interested?" Enough to do violence to pretty little ego? Do you want it as much as air?

3. *"I am looking for fellow-seekers, preferably those who know more than myself."* Who? St. Germain, Master Koot Hoomi, Nostradamus, some famous occultist? Who? Even God can be easily held away. You ought to know, since you are doing it! So what can poor Koot Hoomi or St. Germain or Jesus do?

There are no degrees of attainment, no more or less. It is first a way of technique and discipline, then BOOM!—a discontinuity, an abyss. The mosquito bites the iron ball, the impossible just naturally happens and life is normal.

Your life now is absurd. But the brainwashed one doesn't know it—or shall we say the unfortunate victim of a post-hypnotic suggestion? (These are merely vague illustrations—call off your dichotomizing dogs!) As for "seeking for seeking's sake," that is really odd! Paradox! Better to imagine a $100 bill in your apartment and seek for it all your life. Then there is little danger of finding it! When I "sought" I said, "By God I hope I get it," not, "I shall have fun in the frustrating process."

Alfred says to Richard, "Knock and it shall be opened unto you." Richard says, "No, no, no!" "What's the trouble?" says Alfred. Replies Richard, "There's only one thing to do—screw up the door." Says Alfred, "Why worry? You're all screwed up anyway!"

4. *"You are first a correspondent until I can find what you are."* Don't do this with an animal. You only <u>suspect</u> it is a tiger! Remember, there are two people involved in this—beware of judging. Good thing I am used to this game or I should say toodle-oo and go round the corner with a wave of the hand in farewell. Then how do you "find out"—if ever? Perhaps such a chance will not occur again. Perhaps you are throwing away something inconceivably important. (I don't say you are.) Perhaps you are as much of an idiot as I was at the age of twenty when I missed my chance by pussyfooting.

Are you so sure of what is to be found that you can risk what is <u>offered now</u> for what you may or may not find later? Where is your option, your insurance policy? Meanwhile, what holds <u>me</u> to the task? My eagerness to "save" you? I am more patient than you would be in the same position since I am objective and am willing to wait and see if there is something possible within a reasonable time. But I can't play God. You will yourself.

If you are sure you will find that this is all a mare's nest, then okay—you are safe. But if you are sure, why continue? It seems your position is tragically illogical. If you are of the opinion that there is some chance I am all I have asserted, then why not be smart, play it cozy?

Suppose I say I have a $10,000 bill to give you one day (and I have done more than that!). Do you put such a person on probation, subject to investigation. I wouldn't. I'd play the guy along in every way, especially if I really thought there was a chance he had the mazuma.

5. *"You are making a thousand guesses. Do not guess."* Am I? Perhaps I am trying to elicit responses. How else can I know you? Can I assist a blank piece of paper? If you write me: "Dear Alfred, 16432984156732198765214314142135," is it going to help? I must see you <u>in action</u>. The problem is <u>you</u>, not something vaguely external. So while you write whatever you <u>do</u> write, I find it important as showing where you stand. This standpoint is the gauge.

6. *"Just tell me."* Why not publish it then in some magazine and tell <u>everybody</u>? It is high time! You must see yourself how silly this remark is. But I don't expect you to see how you yourself are providing data by everything you do or say. Ah well!

7. *"You tell God to help you do what you are trying so hard to do."* God is to be sure the essence not only of our quest, but <u>is our quest itself</u>, and our "work" as we do it. But I am not "trying" to do something. <u>I am doing it</u>, and need no help in technique. You will give all the help you are capable of anyway. It may be enough. It may not be.

It is as if I have an instrument, a "state" meter, in my consciousness, and at all times know where the needle points. (On a meter from 10 to 100 your needle points to about 22.) Note that this is a <u>state</u> meter, not a verbal-understanding meter — which is not of the slightest use.

A student's reading may regress a little at times, but there is usually progress as the student exhausts his repertoire of advice, cooperation, disagreement, frustration, suggestions, analysis, summing-up, comparison, reason... All these are strictly for the birds. The state I am interested in is not in these things.

When I was a student myself, while I was "working" with somebody, I was spluttering all the time—just like wise Richard—and mistaking word-meanings (nothing!) for being-state (the criterion). Granted it is curious, frustrating, annoying—but <u>this is how it is</u>. It made me very ill-tempered, I know! You are "working" now, in spite of what you say pro and con.

8. "*Schizophrenia, paranoia*." The seeds of both of these exist in all of us. Paranoia, of course, stems merely from the "boss" conception that ego has of himself. Blown up as big as an ox, he will fancy that he can alter the world, govern nations, order everybody about.

So the humble "awakened" person is accused of paranoia, but he only issues orders "on request" and "by agreement" when a student <u>asks</u> him to do so <u>for a purpose</u>. He does not reform the world or seek power. He is no Richelieu, "*eminence grise*," or power behind the throne. He just lives inconspicuously, and usually dies the same way—unless his disciples blow him up!

Schizophrenia is used as a device by the ego to pretend objectivity. You "seem" to be cooperating with me to process your own self. Thus you are both objective and subjective, apparently. (Two egos!) You attempt to see our work from the outside, to advise, to assess progress, to make modifications, to help me work with you, and so forth. You speak of Richard in a God-like way: "Is he an escapist or a dreamer?" "I saw myself from above the world." "Best wishes for an early success." You are detached in appearance only! This is an ego trick—one of many.

"But," says Richard, "I am not working with

you yet. I first have to know somehow if you have any qualifications whatever. So let me see your stuff."

What stuff? What do you expect—miracles? Well, I have helped in some remarkable things, but they are <u>no more miraculous than anything else</u>! Specifically, I cannot levitate, or turn chalk into cheese, or raise the dead, or even see things at a distance or practice mental telepathy. Apart from them there will be nothing at all, no sign, no evidence. My friends, when they became friends, found there was a *transmission*. They did <u>become sure</u>—but how I don't know. I could switch you to a roshi or to other friends I know who are awakened—if they would take you—but few work this way, maybe none except the commercial rackets. What now?

Friend,
Alfred

P.S. What is the answer? I think it is that the "good soil," or hopeful student, already knows the game somewhat, by <u>instinct</u>. Others try to use judgment and reason and get all conjangulated!

September 23

Dear Richard,

Numeric references are to your letter.

(1) Wit and humor from an E.P. (I shall use "E.P." in future for either Egocentric Person, or Egocentric Predicament or Egocentric Position) are <u>not</u> what they are from an A.P. ("Awakened Person"). The A.P. (and God!) has the outgoing and "sunny" fun which <u>desires not to harm</u>. Don't know what Freud said about wit.

As a weapon, the master—I suppose one has to define the therapist, and since he is temporarily "in control" this term may do, as in Zen master—uses any tool that will do the job, including bitter irony, mordant sarcasm, violent antitheses, and so forth, to throw into relief points that could be overlooked. The end amply justifies such means. About "elevation" I speak again under "Personality of the Master."

(2) *Surely your logic is faulty? Or perhaps you do not have enough data?* I have spent more money than you may ever see at one time in these houses and this property ("land poor") and have been able to retire to devote my life to "this matter." It is difficult work. It was almost (or quite) a miracle that made this possible. So, do you think I wish to engage in an endless series of wrangles in which I am emotionally involved just for the fun of playing God or playing therapist, or satisfying an ego-drive or sadistic impulses? If I am an A.P. I do not get hooked by personality factors. If I am not an A.P. then <u>you</u> are wasting your time.

(3) 50% of my analyses may be wrong, but part of our work is for you to say so. So please take each one where I am "wrong" and explain why. We must

27

appear to tangle, or where is the "transmission"? More briefly: Suppose you wrote a letter of one sentence only: "Alfred, you are 100% wrong." Whatever the truth of this, it would not establish much communication, would it? Our link is only these squiggles on this paper! Thus, more verbiage please, and keep it coming regularly.

(4) Yes, this is the way, to <u>remove egocentricity</u>—but not for the sake of doing so! "Complete details" are, for example, in Karen Horney's *Neurosis and Human Growth*. Do not get this book (no objection to your glancing at it in a bookstore) because one may know it all and still have done nothing. See my encursus on "Ego_1 and Ego_2."

(5) If you say you will work with me:

(a) You must "do as I say" (grant me that power). There is no "penalty," of course, other than one that is <u>inconceivably great</u>—that of "missing the mark." This is not a penalty to <u>you</u> because you do not yet <u>know</u> the "mark." (This is covered under "Personality of the Master.")

(b) Also, as under (3), more verbiage and regularly. See Matthew 10:22, which reads: "...but he that endureth to the end shall be saved."

(c) I should like your promise to not "just" discontinue, but to be man enough to write a letter saying why. Most people slink off with their tail between their legs. It is helpful to know.

This letter is explicit and objective and so are the appendices, "Personality of the Master," and "Ego_1 and Ego_2." However from now on (if you "work" as you say you will) we plunge into entanglement. You will be imputing things to me which are probably not so. My refutations may be wrong, apparently prejudiced and so forth. Annoyance may (and should) mount. It can "clear up" magically at any time and then you would say (without entanglement!), "Of course!"

But right now, speaking to your Ego_1 I say that this is well worthwhile since there is a rare and wonderful thing to win. I say this now as a friend very sincerely. One day we may be friends, but right now I am far too grandmotherly!

Friend,
Alfred

Personality of the Master (the catalyst)

I worked with a Taoist in the succession of classical Taoism — a rare person indeed. However for a man like myself, terribly ego-entangled, like you a smart aleck, this method was too mild. I encountered a lady who had been working as a therapist. I gradually came to think she was far superior for me to the other person, so I switched — feeling remorseful about the Taoist, who is now my friend.

This "exercising of judgment" was an ego thing perhaps, but it was justified by the event. I wish to emphasize that throughout my "work" with both of these people I had no proof that they had any, shall we say, transcendental enlightenment. I conjectured it, but even then it was only words and imagination, because of course I did not know what it was, not having had it myself.

Zen: Zen masters are "guaranteed" to be enlightened by the master that "taught" them (wrong word — but let us not boggle here). This "guarantee" goes back in a chain (uninterrupted, we assume) to the Buddha Gautama, and I have enough details in my library to trace any Zen master all the way back to

Hui-neng and Bodhidharma—and thence to Gautama himself. But who guarantees Gautama?

Christianity: There is no Christian chain like this. Ordination does not confer experience. Only sacrifice does that—and an awakened master. Only rare persons have done it alone, and even then we do not know all the contributing and formative influences. It could happen under the tortures of the Gestapo, but that is rough, dreadfully so. Jesus said, "My yoke is easy." Well, "devotion to God" seems the easiest way and the pleasantest. It would not have done it for me, and I think not for you, sonny boy.

But Jesus was an accomplished therapist, and it appears even through the weird theological trappings of the New Testament. Mark (John Marcus) was a shrewd individual and I suppose was about 50 when he wrote, remembering his boyhood experiences and what Peter said, and Paul, and friends like Luke and relatives like Barnabus. While he wrote, Jerusalem was being destroyed by the Romans, and Jesus told them that would happen if they (the Jews) continued to revolt.

Individual Christians like Eckhart have become enlightened, and then they had to "play it cozy" or get burnt alive. Nevertheless people asked Jesus continually for a sign, and the "Gospels" (John never used the word) contain many "miracles" which are supposed to guarantee his enlightenment. They do not! Jesus himself warned against this.

Subud: "Bapak" Subuh became enlightened in 1933, and without forcing it he has become world-known in "Subud." (It is only a coincidence that the name "Subud" resembles his own: "Subuh.") This method uses physical decontrol, physical surrender, first. It is said to work, although I have not personally met one person enlightened this way.

30

My teacher and I use some physical methods where necessary. Especially with middle-aged and older persons, bodily tensions may be obstacles to "work" and may be holding mental blockages. Thus it may be necessary to supplement psychotherapy with a new kind of physiotherapy — not merely the current meaning of that word, which refers to exercising muscles, the use of prosthetic devices, and so on, but rather "de-control."

Hatha Yoga makes the prime mistake of "controlling." Better to let the body do its work! The "voluntary" muscles etc. cause all your troubles, because friend ego is handling them and "channeling" them. (See F.M. Alexander's work in England and many others.)

Later, I grew to understand my own teacher and to apply the Tibetan word *rinpoche*, meaning honored or revered. She was not in a "chain," and had no teacher. So my "guarantee" goes back to her "guarantee." Thus there is always one not guaranteed.

Taoism: When Lao Tse was asked for credentials he said, "By the Tao." What else is there to say?

Thus a delicate discrimination is required in choosing a master. (Lucky to have a choice!) "Discrimination" is used in the sense of the Sanskrit word *viveka,* which implies "weighing the imponderables." This you must nevertheless do. Almost a leap in the dark. Faith that proof will come! A paradox however you look at it.

Since masters are one-in-a-million, and of those, masters who work by correspondence are one-in-who-knows-how-many, where can you turn? Either to Subud or to the Zen master in New York (Miura Roshi). These, however, require personal attendance, and even then may not be for you. A slim chance indeed! 1 in 3,000,000,000! I doubt exceedingly if any advertised course is worth anything except as a mild psychotherapy or literary sedative, if that.

The student hardly ever thinks that the master <u>knows intimately and as a friend</u> that which is responsible for the trees, the earth, the nebulas, not to mention ourselves! Even if the student regards this as <u>hypothetical</u> he should at least imagine it is <u>how the master sees it</u>—and that therefore a minute squabbling about fancied slights and so forth is out of place in this larger context, and more suitable for children and the highly superficial and moronic. The student should in fact have <u>some</u> of the elements of greatness and fine thinking, otherwise the "work" is as vain, as the French say, as "washing the head of a donkey."

The master must be very patient because the student <u>assumes</u> that he will "stand by" while the student questions, probes and examines—often flippantly and to excess.

The student, by his very experimenting, is showing that he <u>does not know</u> whether the master is one or not! So he should at least make sure that his quarry doesn't get away while he draws a bead on it! Fortunately, the master knows this only too well.

Sokatsu Shaku, on his seventieth birthday (April 16, 1939), recounted to Sokei-An that in the 40 years of his teaching, 3,000 men and women had come to study Zen under his direction. Of these, he initiated 900 (presumably the rest were inaccessible), and of these, 13 completed the training. Of these 13, only 4 had "penetrated to the core of Zen" and became teachers. They were Soseki Goto, Eisan Tatsuta, Chikudo Ghasama and Sokei-An himself. I worked, as I said, under a pupil of Ghasama—and friend of Sokei-An—but changed, as I said. Zen is tough indeed.

"Personality" is a dangerous thing for us to estimate people by. A priest may appear to us to have "elevation" and to be a fine and dedicated man, but there are many such men, and they rarely, very rarely, help towards enlightenment. I declined the title of "Venerable" in the Buddhist church (of Soto Zen), because such things are devices and do not suit me. I belong to no organization.

My "master" could as well have been a bum who found enlightenment under the stars while hitchhiking a ride on an open freight-car, or a man who robbed a bank. In no way do I teach "ethics," although "freedom," curiously enough, leads to conduct that seems highly satisfactory in general, and never tends to "meanness." Thus there are no criteria, and one can easily, as Shakespeare said, be "deceived by ornament" (and by "elevation"). Authors get accepted this way, and also the "princes" of the church, the Pope, bishops, great scientists and psychologists, philanthropists, millionaires, political figures, "famous" persons... Pass them by, for this is Dead Sea fruit.

But the dog of the mind "investigates" every lamp-post—and in plainer English, how hard it is to reject the thousands of fascinating paper-backs and other publications. Yet I might ask you not to read anything of the sort (unless prescribed). Certainly you can have only one master at a time. This is not a case of picking up a trifle here and a trifle there. That you have done so far.

It seems I am drifting from the master to the student so let us do so officially under the caption:
"Ego_1 and Ego_2" (Devices to preserve Egocentricity)

We do not pull flowers up to see how they are growing, but Ego (Self) cannot endure being out of the driver's seat, and so even in the "work" he tries to be both objective and subjective. To be specific, Ego_1 wants to watch the progress of the work with an occasional criticism or pat on the back for the master. "How shall we handle Ego_2?" is asked by Ego_1. Or, "I don't think I (who is "I"?—why Ego_1) would have handled me (Ego_2) quite that way." Or, "Fine," says Ego_1, "that's showing him (Ego_2)." This schizoidal device preserves Ego at the expense of a fictitious Ego_2. You have already started this process.

Sometimes Ego_1 will say he is "seeking" and does not desire to find. What is this? A pleasure merely in the action of the reason? Apparently. In any case Ego_2 is not even necessary here. Ego is asserting the utmost "doubt even of doubt" and refusal to go even as far as the word "the" without definition. It is a sound and invulnerable position. So is advanced psychosis, but that seems more restful—at times! Such a position (like solipsism) is fine when one is healthy, happy, young and immortal. It gets an awful kick later.

Ego_1, for all that, sometimes feels that his constant observation of Ego_2 ("self-consciousness") is unsatisfactory. He may feel that his division is a faked device. In love he may for a time forget himself (which means become spontaneous), and the experience is delightful, unaccustomed, and turns out often to be most unwise. It occurs often when young and when judgment would be desirable (for a change), especially if the girl is not so spontaneous! If they both are, it is wonderful. But again the claims of the everyday come in, and the magic fades away.

Everything in Japan used to be a "way." There

was a "way" of sword-play, of wrestling, of flower arrangement, of drinking tea, of commerce even, of drawing and painting—and the characteristic of each was spontaneity. Even archery (incredible results even in semi-darkness, splitting one arrow with another)— and such spontaneity daunts us. We are system-minded. Zen may seem to be a "system" of mass-production, but the essence of the work is <u>individual</u>.

I have no "system" whatever, for the same reason—no two people are alike. Certainly egocentricity is always the devil to be conquered, but from that central point, he (ego or self) diverges in innumerable ways and uses every imaginable device—some very snide, others really subtle. He may know it, too—and still throw up a smoke-screen! He resists the means to release—to the point of murder even. Fortunately, since he is free to withdraw at any time, he usually withdraws under a confusion of self-justification. But if he were trapped—as I was—oh boy! In the Reichian technique, for example, the room is often a shambles.

So we do "protect" something—and how! What? Ego? Oh no—while we live we are, of course, "we," and always that remains. But the "boss" conception, the "ultimate decider," the "second line of defense," these he protects and insists on at all costs.

So Jung and others know the truth but sit in the audience (behind their desk for example) and are never part of the play. It is ludicrous to think I could help Jung—he is heavily armed. I could get one letter from almost everybody by promising "a new technique," but to get involved in it—oh dear no! Most certainly not! Utterly fantastic who-knows-what!

Thus Jesus was correct. It is the treasure of the <u>humble</u>, and for this goodly pearl a merchant sold all he had—and bought it. I can persuade almost anybody to say, "Okay, go ahead! What do I have to lose?" But it is a Pyrrhic victory, unreal. In that way one sells toothpaste. They must come to me and <u>really want it</u>. Since they can easily push God away, how can I succeed where God does not? This is not a mystery I can solve. But the truly accessible, as Jesus said, are few. Up to you.

So many words!

Alfred

Dear Richard,

You have understood me very clearly. We have given a name to our problem — egocentricity. You have this disease and I see you have it. I am the doctor and have cured cases before. So the thing to do is clear — cure it. And you "thank me for my efforts." And you say that prior to my last letter you "made statements" and my treatment consisted in saying "you are full of bologna."

(a) You make the widest (and truest!) generalization: "The master knows that one too," but in detail you are (probably of necessity, my poor friend) forced to act against your own words because you are trying to watch the process of your own deliverance! Hence the "analysis," like above (knocking down all statements).

But if what you say were true, then any Tom, Dick or Harry — and in particular the one that is you, could set up in business as an A.P. ("Awakened Person"), and have an orgy of destruction, name-calling, epithet-inventing, and so forth, while looking hopefully to curing his dupes. But, physician heal thyself! It might not work. In rare cases it might, but, oh boy, what a mess — what a fight! However, there are quite a number of people who do habitually act this way — in a mild degree Groucho Marx, Alexander King, Alexander Wolcott — in fact most intellectuals, especially those just emerged from the egg — and even you with your "dialectical attack" and "analytical affront" on the fairer and pleasanter sex.

Everything above may be true and we may both know it. "The master knows that one too," however, means that he can thread his way with ease and assurance in the most god-awful tangle the ingenious mind can throw up!

Your whole letter, as I said, is really excellent. You get involved here and there, and of course you feel it, and you say, very naturally, "What the hell!" But here are cases where you try to go further as in (a) above and investigate my technique:

(b) *"I presume anything I might say would be superfluous. So I keep my words to a minimum."* The second sentence is very true and honest. Often people say "I can find nothing to say to you." They can go to someone else and deliver themselves of 25,000 assorted words on the same subject! Literary men say often, "I have no ideas and stare at a blank page." Wow! Again, they have millions (and can breed more at that), but they are not satisfied with what they have, so they clam up.

Thus you put your finger on it, "I keep my words to a minimum." But "I" is at the moment my enemy—the enemy of Alfred! So I say—do not do so. So, talk! Orders! You say, "But I don't wanna talk." That is your disagreeable task and you have my sympathy! Ub-gub doesn't help!

Your first sentence, "I presume…" shows the first wound to the ego. It hurts. He retreats. That is all. But such a "light affliction" can "win so great a prize." (Christianity has all the words somewhere.)

(c) *"I do understand that you may be trying to clarify my thinking processes."* Not at all. They are perfectly clear and pellucid as is. We shall use them—even against themselves—but my aim is otherwise. "Thinking" is a barren desert. Even so-called psychological integration demands a fusion of thinking and feeling. You may not even be able to define "feeling."

"Intuition" is on the intellectual or thinking

side still. Nor will "imagination" help! It falls short, of course. Define "feeling," "intuition" and "imagination," and see if they can help and how much.

So much for a general analysis of the position (in cold blood) and for (a), (b), (c), where the student attempts to divine the process and to help it along.

I have asked some questions and suggested some things to examine. These will give you pegs to hang your discourse upon. But you asked some questions, too! So:

"What will happen to money, houses, farm, wife when the universe goes up in smoke?" (What will happen to you and me anyway, eventually?) This is a Zen koan and the master does not attempt to answer it verbally. He may — as regards himself, say — remark that he will be on his back with his face to the sky or variants of this.

(1) "Psychic research" and the less respectable religion of Spiritualism attempt to answer this. So does the Western group of religions and some of the Eastern ones (like Shin-shu and its "happy Western land" presided over by Amida or Amithaba who helps us to the "awakening" we have missed on earth).

(2) So does Theosophy and the school of rebirth, transmigration and reincarnation. These things, (1) and (2), are not very compatible! Researchers try to get messages through — via a medium — from their loved ones deceased, but rarely look around in society to find where their loved one has "reincarnated." Of course there may be a longer time between incarnations. As a factual matter, Spiritualism fights reincarnation — and so does Christianity.

This is your only real question and so I must

comment on some statements you make.

"I do not know what you mean by guarantee. Did you trust your Hindu 'master'? Or were there reservations?" Long before I "got anywhere" I sensed what my teacher was and had. It is essential, even if it does not immediately "do what has to be done." In the "Buddha" Gautama, men sensed a curious plus-value, and evidently in Jesus there was "something" beyond normal personality, even though the disciples may have maintained the idea that he was some sort of a "Messiah" and a wonder-worker.

Transcendence goes beyond miracles and all phenomena. If you only find my "personality" you will have found nothing unusual. It is as "unique" as yours is, or for that matter anything in nature whatever, since we all pick up different odds and ends for our memory-boxes as we live and experience. As such it is interesting, but so is your own. The "wonderful thing" is <u>not unique</u>! It is not prized for its unusual nature as compared with other things. It is <u>common to all</u>, even if buried under metaphorical tons of rubble.

"Masks." We seek what is common to all, not what is unique. You mention "personalities" or "faces." All are "real," as such, and that is awkward, isn't it? Listen to a man's voice change as he gets a female voice on the phone, or a salesman trying to sell him a Canadian copper-mine stock, or an old friend, or his wife, or a priest, or his boss, or a child...

So we ask, "How in the name of God does he talk when alone?" Try it. Feels awkward doesn't it? Afraid of two men in white with a butterfly net? You can always talk to "God"! But apart from the fact that you do not know what you are addressing (and what language It talks!), it would involve <u>sincerity</u>—and that is very tiring, rather objectionable. Similarly, when we lose memory (amnesia). Then there is confusion.

Do we have "one" something? Oh yes! Ever since you became self-conscious (awakening No. 1) as a child you have had this. It is overlaid but recoverable. I do not say that this process (of recovering the *puer aeternitatis*) is directly a technique for awakening, but it has a relation to it, as has envisaging the same thing in the master.

As far as the student is concerned, the work is <u>not</u> to "improve" his Goddamn <u>understanding</u>! Charmingly fatuous (the sweet odor of decay). If you will allow me to make reference to God, I would put it that this will not help you as far as God is concerned! "Look! Me Richard. Me smart boy, no?" No. Christ Jesus. Oh well. One thing you cannot fool.

"The Egocentric Person." You have as many spikes as an ancient "mace," or as the spiked sphere (centrosome) which is crucial to mitosis (cell-division)—and which, by the way, calmly divides and "sits" one on each side of the nucleus of the cell-to-be-split! Such spikes are the obstacles to being a warm, high-minded human-being. The true process of awakening therapy is more like house-breaking a cat, or explaining to an "underprivileged" child that there are good reasons why he should not casually expectorate on the carpet.

The pride of an Einstein or a Sir Julian Huxley or a C.G. Jung or an Erich Fromm (who already "know it all") would not endure such a process for one moment. I know. And add the "urbane" (well-armed) third Earl Russell, Bertrand Russell, under whom I once studied briefly. Such humor, such Ajax-like "resting on a foundation of unyielding despair." And that of course suggests Sartre, who has made a good thing out of plays, articles, books—on that same "despair." Not only are you in numerous company but, as these names show, in excellent company!

"*The master.*" As for "envisaging the same thing in the master," Zen calls this "*the transmission.*" Words do not "transmit" it, but negatively they can show the way. Tangents may define a curve, although not one tangent is part of the curve—in this case a spiral. (Although I am a mathematician I have forgotten the word for "the curve which is enveloped by tangents." There is a word.) Neti. Neti. "Not this way." As Lao-Tse says, "Men love by-paths." More accurately, ego seeks at every moment the easy by-path that corresponds to his inclination and makes him "purr." One must go against this tendency and ignore dotted line alternatives.

Am I speaking vaguely and "generally"? Oh no! Each dotted line (in my diagram) represents an occasion where the student fights by one means or another. He "changes" the subject under discussion to a more "satisfactory" one, he ignores a remark, he counterattacks ("Let's stop squabbling." "Say something definite." "We are not getting anywhere." "What I would do is… " "You don't understand me." "Most of what you say is wrong."), or he withdraws.

When you say, "You are making a thousand guesses," I would naturally say, "Give three." Guessing at what?" Need I "guess" when you can enlighten me so easily? So, please give three. (However, you may have changed a little since you wrote that. But "there is nothing hidden that shall not be revealed." (Curious statement—but I mean it literally—don't hint, talk out.)

This is not a contest. The usual dirty fighting of everyday intercourse doesn't go. This is not for my benefit. When I was myself "working" there was also physical "work" (which you are spared), and here

42

ego's shrieks rose to a crescendo, so to say!

You may say, "Have I got to keep putting my chin up for your fist?" To that I would say—if that were true and the "way," then: "Yes, by all means." But actually you have a certain "nature" right now. It needs to be changed—"know thyself."

Psychoanalysis goes into minute detail but no synthesis appears even after five years. Other therapies are usually gentle—and so very long. No doubt a kid-glove technique might be possible, but with the same result requires the same pain—either to take the tooth out with one yank or to play with it for hours!

The Gestapo of SS men would be ideal—but maybe too much for our purposes! We need to desensitize ego. These urbane and polished people, and many others, have actually a raw and inflamed ego that cannot bear the gentlest touch. If a waiter says, "Not that fork, sir," they would never recover. Actually the pain is absurd and quite unreal. In business some pretty crude terms are used (tricky old son-of-a-bitch, and so forth) but a smile makes them a compliment. Suppose there were no smile?

The ego does not surrender *in vacuo*. There are attendant circumstances. Otherwise it would be open, theoretically, for the most unlikely people to "go over the hump" all of a sudden. However, intelligence is requisite—even cunning, or discrimination (which sounds better). Also the highest of standards, a deep love of beauty (although not of a "formal" nature— you will know what I mean, no pretentious yak-yak), so that the "change-over" occurs because for a moment you are already there anyway. That is why "bhakti," or devotion, is considered so good a "way" by the Hindus (and myself, since if "bhakti" is sufficiently pure it is the very experience we seek).

I am really speaking of "feeling" as additional to "knowing," of "spontaneity" as opposed to a "system." I am speaking of a <u>full</u> man.

If you asked for examples (now living) I could give no more than a couple dozen of my own knowledge. If you ask, "Do you regard me, Richard, as a yahoo?" I would say, "I rank you with the great ones of the earth, the great psychologists, scientists, etc., the most perceptive, scholarly, charming, kindly men." If you then said, "In other words, a yahoo," it would be embarrassing! After all, between them such persons have all the virtues, a wonderful personality, great kindness, a fine appearance—and so why this pejorative comparison with a mere horse? Well, I didn't do it—it was Swift.

For our first aim then, let us see if we can agree. Not verbally, because that is a mere nothing, but in detail. Thus you would investigate, analyze or attack vigorously anything not clear—but use legitimate arguments (not devices).

You would also agree not to withdraw until I say there is no more to be done. Any specific requests I make you would follow.

"*Yoga.*" "Joining" what is already one! Quite a trick. If we "decide" to meditate we have one strike against us! Besides, it is a do-it-yourself technique. Those are only for heroes. How to decide not to decide? Wu-wei. Hatha Yoga seeks to control. You control more than you can handle (in the body) already. You need to <u>decontrol</u>.

"*We cannot follow science and intuition.*" Intuition is the method of science. I feel you regard "intuition" as a higher faculty than it is. It is only short-cut thinking, and does not include ESP and other methods—or alleged methods—of direct knowledge. In other words, if intuition represents your advance upon "intellection," it is a trifling one, and in the same field. What do you think "intuition" is?

"Nothing." In many of your letters you voice the curious fear that you might become a "nothing." The fact is that you are now a nothing—but you can become a "something." Another metaphor is the top of a submerged iceberg (7/8 under water)—and I do not mean the "subconscious."

You can have "attachment" and anything else you like after you have done what is needful. I am not suggesting your way of life—only the way to being able to "live." The "cast" is while the broken leg heals, not the normal way of living. I am not prescribing ways of life—I am trying to work a change-over experience. You confuse means with ends! The scaffolding is not the skyscraper. Questions about what you are and where you go have no place in the "work" we are doing, which is to free you to judge and act (or at least to know whether it is "you," or what it is).

Jesus and Gautama and others elaborated a philosophy from their understanding. So have I. So could you. But to use it to get understanding is ridiculous. Hence the folly—utter folly—of reading books on philosophy, etc. (And that cuts out thousands of enticing old and new issues.)

      Friend,
      Alfred

Note: First stage: "Normalcy." Dissatisfaction, frustration—no way out seen. Second stage: "Working." More frustration, as this seems still more pointless and leading nowhere. Rebellion. Far too austere. Third stage: Period of change-over. Satori.

Satisfaction handed to you on a platter. Oh boy. Hope it lasts for ever. (It doesn't.) <u>Fourth stage</u>: Truly normal living. After some months, however, (or a year) of "digestion," you seem to yourself the same as before, i.e. normal. Men find you pleasant, maybe, no more than that. But... No questions!

Dear Richard,

I do not remember past lives. I do not know if I had any or will have future ones. I can not levitate, and even if I could it would prove something with regard to gravity, but nothing transcendental. It is desirable not to lose oneself in this field of magic and the false "occult."

Your "sifting among many of the world's religions" would not help you unless you recognized that they did not spring from an extension of primitive fertility rites (both sex and agriculture!), but rather, around BC 850 - 500, from individuals who brought direct experience into the various practices so well described by anthropologists like Frasier, Haddon (under whom I studied) and others.

Such individuals were Jesus, Gautama, Lao Tse, Moses, etc. They could not verbalize their "experience," but they did say something—which was a compromise, and thus containing popular, crude and in fact false elements along with some hints of what they could not put into words.

They described the mystery they found as God, Brahman, the Tao, Jehovah and so on. Names merely. Only in experience is the meaning or "referent" known. So this is what they found.

The next question is how they found it, and how others can find it. Again there is unanimity world-wide. No amount of examination of the outside world, scientific or otherwise, will do. Every discovery man makes leads him only to the next—and so on without end. Molecules to atoms to protons to mesons—and whatever smaller thing will come next. Planets to suns to galaxies to a universe—fascinating and endless. In fact, the "nature" of things is never arrived at. We find that all is "energy" or "mind," but cannot define such things.

Thus the search is <u>into oneself</u>: "Know thyself." It has been found all over the world, in all ages, that the self acts as an obstacle to the Light coming in. Can we remove the self? No! Only by dying. But the self in itself is not the real obstacle. It is the fierce contention of the self that it is the final court of appeal, the final judge, the "owner" of the organism, the boss, and so forth.

It was found that to remove this deciding and judging function by a decision or a judgment is ridiculous because we cannot decided not to decide — because we are still "deciding" even in that. Problem!

So people tried austerity, starvation, flogging themselves, sitting in meditation and contemplation so as to forget or drop the deciding function — and then found that they were still deciding to be austere, to meditate and so forth! It is like trying to lift oneself up by one's own bootstraps, or to see one's eye, or for a sword to cut itself. Jesus said, "With man it is impossible."

However, it wasn't impossible with Jesus or Gautama, and some few others may have had such a strong impulse that little was needed to produce abnegation of the self and surrender of the "I" which leads to the "experience" (of satori, of awakening, of "seeing and knowing God directly").

Yet for all other people, who are not such heroic figures, a master or guru is necessary. His function is to help the student to surrender, to the removal of ego-domination, of "bossiness." Just as we need an outside point to rest a lever on if we are to move the earth (as Archimedes said), so we need a friend to help our ego-fight from an exterior point of view from ourselves.

It is necessary that this master be <u>awakened</u> himself, because this is not a mechanical system, and this mystery, this "God," is very much alive, conscious, and directs the process (and everything else) even though in the student it is still hidden. (Our little consciousness hides this big Consciousness like a penny hides the Sun.)

Since the ego must be dethroned in the student, it is a disagreeable, unsatisfying, hard, up-hill process all the way.   Why? Because the definition of "agreeable," "pleasant," etc. is what we like, what we want, what the "I" desires, what makes it "purr" and happy! But we wish to act <u>against</u> it—it is our enemy while it has the boss-complex. It must realize it is an efficient executive officer but not the boss.

Thus the student must do as the master says, and agree to do so while the "work" lasts. (Even with a psychotherapist or surgeon or doctor you are in this position.) The "master" does not enjoy this task, except in so far as the result is so wonderful if achieved. He is not a sadist. He is not doing this to satisfy his impulses for domination, and so forth. The reason is of course that he has been through the mill himself and has had that knocked out of him—it is the very ego-domination we are discussing. Thus, you must <u>only</u> work with an "awakened" person.

Now, the Zen masters are "guaranteed," so to say, each by their own master all the way back to the "Buddha" Gautama (via Hui Neng and Bodhidharma). I accept this, although I do not know the precise nature of their satoris. There is one master in New York—Miura Roshi—but one has first to become a Buddhist properly, and then to "work" with him personally. There is no easy way, no "royal road."

I myself wish to help everybody, but it is no

use "casting pearls before swine, <u>as they will turn and rend you</u>"! I try to reach those who are ready and "accessible" to this "work," but at present I have few correspondents and some of those will, I think, drop away. So what is of the <u>greatest value</u> in the whole universe is <u>not desired</u>! Jesus said he "found all men asleep." He might have added, "and they resist being awakened."

I myself recognized the extreme value of this "work" and was very fortunate in finding a brave teacher. I was as obstinate and "smart alecky" as you, and for a little coconut I talked very big, as do you.

Now you can buy paperbacks and other books that have all sorts of fascinating and glittering insights and marvels. You can meet remarkable and interesting people, have many more-or-less good "friends," have interesting hobbies and professions or avocations, join various societies and organizations, but I doubt very much if this will ultimately satisfy you or content your restlessness. If it does, well and good.

People wish to sit on their fannies and languidly toy with some doctrine or other. Their contribution in time and attention is the minimum. A push-button system or a pill is their ideal. <u>Sacrifice</u> is not even contemplated, but it is the <u>only way</u>. There is a price-tag on everything, and to get all you must <u>give all</u>. For less you only get a substitute.

My position is a difficult one. I cannot look for students, or persuade them, because I cannot debauch or debase this great thing by huckstering and advertising methods. But I do wish to meet those who earnestly seek a teacher or master to help them. Such people exist (I was one myself), but most people have been so solicited by creeds and organizations and TV advertising that they are languid and demanding.

As for "famous" and well-known men and

women, they are kept from the truth by the adulation they receive, and rarely have genuine humility. Jesus said this, and it is so. (Hidden from the "wise" and revealed to the simple.) Nicodemus came to him secretly, by night, and even then was hopelessly confused, as are you — or <u>pretend</u> to be.

I have, however, stated the facts so that a child could understand them (and shall not restate them). To humble oneself and find God is all. I will not dangle a carrot by giving you the advantages of the "awakened" life and the dangers of the normal life. If you were a personal friend I met every day, or a relative, I should probably be biased enough by affection to stress these things. But you have not yet become a friend, and I have not even your photograph. And so you are one of 3,000,000,000 people, of whom most are obstinate, dangerous, and unreliable when tested ever so slightly. Indeed, they are on the verge of the most awful agony the world (and you) have ever known.

Your letter is mostly dialectic, cool intellectual discussion, and seems to get us no further. How do you expect to "understand" me ultimately? To understand me you would have to have arrived at a certain point yourself. Lao Tse says exactly that. But then so did Jesus. In the parable of the sower he mentions the various types of people and the way they "understand" him — some like good ground for the "seed" he sowed, some shallow ground, some rocks.

There are very few awakened people around. The horseman rides past the window. One glance — or you have missed seeing. In later life this could be recognized as a major tragedy. Suppose I was trying to give away a $10,000 bill. Should I hold somebody down, tie his hands and shove it in his pocket and then sew it up? How foolish can people be?

Friend,
Alfred

Dear Richard,

"Evasive" would imply that I am avoiding deliberately (since my eyes are supposed to be wide open) a logical or reasonable reply to your questions and remarks. So let me take all your specific questions as a minimum and segregate the topics, thus:

(1) *God*. Why did I choose this particular word? (You and I know it is semantically precarious and carries a heavy "charge" of meaning, put there by theological know-it-alls.)

(a) Well, first, what is the origin of the word? The Jews used Jahweh (or at least JHVH leaving the vowels to be forgotten as the name was taboo). Jesus used "Abba" (Father) in Aramaic. The Jews also used Adonai (Lord), Elohim and other words. "God" is not cognate with "good," apparently, and is some old German or Gothic deity, now obsolete. He may have had a wife, and may have required weird rituals. I wish I knew more of his origin!

However, some names for the One are very impersonal and ineffable, like the Tao (Way), the Brahman, the Dharmakaya, etc. Others are personal like Allah, Jehovah (Yahveh), God, Krishna, Siva, Brahma (the masculine member of the Brahman trinity — there is one temple to him, none to the Brahman), Chemosh (the god of the Moabites who amuses me by his name somehow, as also Lord Dunsany, and to whom Solomon made a "high place" outside old Jerusalem, but who was a bloodthirsty old ruffian — worse than Jehovah if possible) — and so forth.

The first group we naturally call "It" (including the "Absolute"). The second group we naturally call "He." "She" is rarer—Isis, Diana, Kali, etc.

Ineffable deities. I find in practice that I have a harder time with Buddhists, for example, because they will exchange ego's pride for their ineffably ineffable. Since the ineffably ineffable is so remote they, too, become inaccessible, since ego has pitched his goal deliberately (!) out of reach, inconceivably. He jumps right over the horse! "He" means a Buddhist student e.g. whose "Dharmakaya" is very remotely ineffable (like the word "Absolute").

Manlike deities. Conversely the Jews, Christians etc. have an anthropomorphic "God," whatever they say to the contrary. In practice he reflects their anger, frustration, sadism, weariness, and so forth. They jump short of the horse!

We want to jump right on the horse, of course. Now since the One Self is intimately associated with us—although not on a "personality" basis—I have less trouble pulling the Jews and Christians up a bit, than pulling the Buddhists, Taoists, Hindus, intellectuals, philosophers, etc. down a bit—a big bit!

It's a practical matter. Ego can take a delight in being very subtle, very occult, very ineffable, whereas the primitive religionist can be too childish, affectionate, etc., instead of child-like, simple, loving.

Puer atternitatis. One obstacle is world-weariness, adult cynicism, etc., which blurs the child-self you must recover. If I were a primitive religionist you could reject this (and me) very easily. But I am not! I am at least your equal, my fine friend.

As an example, there is a bad mistranslation in the New Testament—it is really stupid. The result is that a tense interchange between Jesus and Peter is converted into a mere question and answer three times repeated pointlessly! It is John 21, verses 15-17.

Love or affection. Jesus asks Peter "Do you love me? (agapaw). Peter answers, "You know I love you" (filew). Non-emotion (Jesus) versus emotion (Peter). Again Jesus asks: "Do you *love* me?" (agapaw--with emphasis). Peter says, "You know I love you (filew). The third time Jesus asks tactfully and sadly, "Do you love me?" Peter says ,"Lord, you know everything. You know I love you (filew).

There are two kinds of love, (agapaw), which is the Love I call "God," and (filew), a personal and mechanical love, which can turn to hate even. When I said "friendship" to you I meant "agapaw" which is outgoing, eternal (and since it is "God" himself, or itself, in us it is truly "eternal.")

Happy are the people who know this rare and wonderful thing below personality level! It can exist between two people of the same sex—David and Jonathan—or between a man and woman. In the latter case it overrides "sex." "Sex" is its conscious servant and supremely natural. Then the man and woman are equals and their association ("married" in the customary sense or not) is a "sacrament" in some old and genuine usage of this term. The woman is not merely a convenient receptacle for a sex organ, and intercourse does not lead to satiety. Alas, this is rare indeed. It can be a young man or woman's ideal, but they usually settle for less.

Here then is the "love" of two child-selves (wise as serpents and innocent as babes), and it truly reflects the Source of the Universe for which I used so obsolete and curious a word ("God").

The English "Revised Version" of 1884 notes in margin, "Peter twice uses a different Greek word than Jesus." (Not much help to a casual reader.) Maurice Nicholl in *The New Man* (1955) deals with it in detail. The *Twentieth Century New Testament* (1900) catches it, and uses "love" as said by Jesus, and "I am your friend" as said by Peter (but that is incorrect as "friend" is merely the wrong use of that word we all make). The *New Testament in Basic English* (1941) also catches it and uses "love" in Jesus' first two questions and "you are dear to me" as Peter's replies.

Since very likely you do not know this "heightened awareness" (agapaw) but only the emotion (filew) you have <u>no referent</u> to "God." You must naturally discard all semantic overtones. This love (agape) "loves" the personality for what it is, good or bad, pleasant or unpleasant, as a mother loves an erring son.

(1) *God (cont.)*

(b) *"What do you want to define as friendship?"* It is the state previously illustrated in detail. It is the "transmission" of Zen. It is when each is "open" with the other. It is an approach of the One Self in each. It is a <u>way to realization</u>. It demands a certain discrimination and a certain culture. A trigger-happy "hood," a sadist, a chawbacon, a "fishwife," an autocratic boss, a proud intellectual, the Pope — all these can easily have a "mystic experience" or "cosmic consciousness" (even though they might call it "only subjective"), but not so easily the "awakening" experience which Jesus said is denied to them and reserved for simple people.

(c) *"What difference does it make whether or not we come to know God?"* Nothing and everything. This is a paradox to make the angels weep! Since you <u>are</u> God and nothing else, it is God <u>realizing himself</u> in this time-space episode. Thus, if you <u>do</u> wish to know God, then it can be an <u>urgent desire</u> (beauty, music, Nature, love, etc., are fingers pointing the way). In that case, "you do," and we should continue. If you <u>do not</u> wish to awake, then clearly that is an alternative situation and we should not continue.

There is no ought, should, must. There is no reason, preference, etc. I do not dangle carrots before the donkey's nose (you), although I could. The Old Testament says, "I put you before Life and Death." "Nature" is indifferent. <u>Refusal</u> to know God (as opposed to ignorance that it can be done) can lead to a quicker "end," and then you can nourish the trees and flowers, and eventually recombine somehow. As Shakespeare says, "Mighty Caesar dead and turned to clay, may stop a hole to keep the winds away."

Why is this? Because "refusal" is an ego phenomenon. About 90% of you is autonomous (fortunately), and the blood circulation, digestion, involuntary muscles, glandular secretions, body repairs, cell growth and division, etc. go on even in sleep, regardless of "Richard" (great and mighty one — perhaps). The other 10% is "your" apparent decision. Thus your stomach may be saying, "Please, please, no more sugar, or fat foods, or carbohydrates," or whatever is wrong at the moment, but your hand may shove more and more of it in your mouth! One is involuntary, one is "voluntary" (in a sense).

Further, ego "channels" your modes of action and response, leading to tensions and local lack of circulation. These can be deadly, and one day the thing (your body) "gives" at the weakest spot. Then there is a "disease" or something and it has a name. It may be "cured," but the underlying condition remains.

Doctors do not have the weeks, months and years of time required to "work" your body to get rid of the predisposing condition. This is not occult or in question. They have been in preparation for a long, long time. The same applies to the mind. It is a delicate instrument and statistics show that one in three are either treated for a mental trouble by a psychotherapist of some sort or are put in an institution. In a less degree there are doubts, conflicts, frustrations and so forth. A man who has "enlightened self-interest" would be a great big fool not to consider such a situation.

However, it is a good time now for you to make up your mind. I am doing some of the work of a psychotherapist and then going far beyond him. However, we are alike in that I and he have to <u>change</u> you—not present ideas to you. He gets $25 or $30 an hour or 40 minutes, and since he doesn't want to kill the goose that lays the golden eggs, he goes suavely and slowly—three years, five years… Of course you may have an anxiety complex and it is either your psychoanalyst or the river. Then you are hooked. Otherwise he doesn't want to lose you, unless you are a really messy piece of goods.

My case is different. It takes me a lot of time and trouble to write to you (this letter is in great detail so as not to seem unnecessarily "evasive"), and naturally you are no different than anyone else. Nor can I work with too many people at this rate, obviously. So if you are merely going along for the ride, having intellectual exercise and all that, I would appreciate you saying that your interest is slight—and thanks and good-bye. That would avoid a hundred more letters, each taking several hours (if that many were necessary. It might be far less—and often has been).

Since I wish to "work" faster than the psychotherapist I have of necessity to be "rougher" in handling your precious ego, just as concentrated soup is saltier and over-flavored until diluted.

(1) *God (cont.)*

(d) *"How do you know that which you experienced*

was God?" Here is the joke of the year, and you will, I hope, see the fantastic nature of the question if I ask you to define "God" first! (And I have every right to do so, since you are asking me.) I do know that what I experienced was <u>not</u> anything I or you has ever seen defined as God—or heard so defined. <u>It was entirely new and entirely different.</u>   So why do I call it God? For this reason. It appears from the accounts and attempted descriptions of men in all ages and all countries—Gautama, Jesus, Eckhart, Heraclitus, Plato, Plotinus, and innumerable other sources (I have a shelf full, for example)—that they and I did have an experience which is like a fully conscious version of the "mystical experience" (which millions have a taste of!). Thus it cannot be called "unconscious"! Further, my teacher had the same, and the Zen and Taoist masters passed it on to their students, too, down the ages.

This experience lead to the great religions (except Islam and Christianity, which are later derivatives of Judaism) that began about BC 850 - 550, superseding the animism and crude fertility rites—often with human or animal sacrifice. (Judaism never got out of it—at least not until much later.)

It was not an evolution! There was a world-wide upsurge of these "awakened" men! It was a "discontinuous" phenomenon, and not explicable by the methods of the anthropologist.

Each of these men spoke of One Source, and their knowledge of how it expresses itself through us both as human organisms and, curiously enough, simultaneously as our apparently "outside" perceptions—in other words, the Universe. Many words which I have already quoted (Tao, The Brahman, etc.) were used to describe this. One is "God."

I will stress that their followers made an unholy mess of what these remarkable men said (the Buddha even said they would!), and this mess you call "religion." I have tried to avoid starting a new one, but in lectures in Taiwan, for example, I hear my poor efforts spoken of as "something new in Asia." Heaven help us! Another one? Subuh in Java was "awakened" in 1933, and here again "Subud" may develop into one of these movements, alas. The fact is people love marvels and magic—which they substitute for the transcendental! (I shall show you do too!)

Thus, "God" is the name of my experience, not that my experience was "of God."

First Richard must know what the experience is, then that it is (and was) world-wide to a few, and finally he can call it anything he pleases.

This answers (partly) your question, *"What do you mean by 'awakening'?"* The answer is that, like Buddha, I cannot explain it to you now, but I can tell when you or others have it, because then it is entirely possible to explain it to one who also knows it. The Zen master can tell by the mere look on the student's face. I have had many curious expressions from students when they "awoke," and very obvious ones to me.

Further, with all due deference to your sensibilities, they were much better human beings than you are now. I asked for your photograph not to stimulate friendship (!), but to know a little more about you. If you came to see me you might know a little more about me, but don't do that at the present stage.

Your questions have been answered, so about the rest of your letter. *Reincarnation.* I was very clear about this, and my comment that people rarely (except in India!) look around to see where a "loved one" has "reincarnated" meant (as it would to any half-perceptive person) that people do not believe in it, obviously. Common sense would tell you that. Their actions prove it. Besides, your body gets scattered and certainly doesn't "reincarnate." So what does? <u>Body and mind are not separable</u>. They go and you know it. However, I do not dogmatize on "life after death," since you must first find out for yourself by "awakening" what our position is, then, armed with this information, you may consider life after death for <u>yourself</u>. First understand "life."

Marvels and miracles. "A person who 'knows God directly' should know whether he has had past lives or future ones." Such questions as to what I <u>should</u> know are best answered by considering the experience of the race of human-beings since they were reasonably conscious — and it could be five or ten thousand years. In this time the race found that the sun rises every morning, that we cannot levitate, that we cannot see at a big distance usually and at will (although curious cases do occur), that we cannot yet change chalk into cheese (except via a cow or complicated chemical work, since we need nitrogen and hydrogen, for example, for cheese and they are not in the chalk), that we cannot usually and at will foretell the future (although curious cases do occur), and so on.

Future experience may add to our knowledge, but as of now, human beings — you and I — have the above limitations. It is not my object to assist you to these powers, which I do not have myself (note all the qualifying words), since I am a humble, limited human-being like everybody I meet. Certainly I would like you to be more of a human-being, but even this is hard to explain to you now.

Consider an underprivileged child from a poor neighborhood being suddenly — by adoption, for example — transported to a wealthy and cultured milieu. It would perhaps be necessary to tell him not to "pick his nose and eat it," or not to spit on the carpet, and a few other trifles he might overlook.

One could tell the kid that he would be one day a distinguished and cultured man, mixing in all societies, but it would be hard to <u>explain</u> the difference there would be in him (as he now is).

When I work with students they are cynical, suspicious, unkind, mean-minded (e.g. they could say, "You are taking all this trouble just because you like teaching and showing off. Well, I will make it hard for you!"), low-motived, not too perceptive, not too intelligent, not too friendly (every now and then I have to dodge a metaphorical knife in my back, and Jesus was tortured to death in an atrocious way while Peter and company considered the matter with gaping mouths and expectation of flocks of angels and big celestial boom-booms — no feeling for their "friend") and so forth.

It is an "occupational hazard." The psychotherapist has the same hazard (e.g. suicidal and homicidal cases), but even he cannot take his patients further than he has gone <u>himself</u> (except by accident — and I have known such), and so he himself has a point at which he would revert to a louse!

I ought to know! I was a student once myself. I am not much better now, but I am a trifle kinder and a trifle more perceptive, maybe!

If I were in the pulpit of a big cathedral, or in the Zendo of a (and as a) Zen master, nobody would think I had thrown a plate at my wife that morning or done a few other disgusting things in private. Thus, as Shakespeare says, "The world is oft deceived by ornament." The profession, the position, gives elevation, and the "sheep" probe no deeper. But perhaps you and I can indulge in the business of the <u>truth</u> about ourselves and humanity.

However, it is also the truth that if this thing we are doing is false, then there is absolutely no <u>other</u> hope for you, me, or humanity — unless Spiritualism or E.S.P. meets your deeper needs. We are not animals, we are human beings with some consciousness, and that is a deep mystery. We are perhaps puppets. We are perhaps even "nothing." But we are "nothings" than can be "something."

So make up your mind. If I ask for a photograph, send it. It is the least you can do. And further, I do not know of any way you can escape from your frustrating ego-domination except by voluntarily giving powers to some other person — me or another if you can find him or her — which will involve your obedience. I had to do it. I know no other way.

Friend,
Alfred

P.S. In this world you do not get something for nothing — there is always a price-tag. And in this case it is "sacrifice." I must say the price is very reasonable considering the merchandise. Yet people would rather die than know the truth. That means that ego is so obstinate that he would rather be extinguished than step down! There are 3,000,000,000 like that.

Dear Richard,

Call the object of our discussion the "One" if you like — it has nothing to do with your frenzied semantics. All the people you mention have only a fancied referent and must be completely disregarded. If they are cuckoo there is no reason for you to be. I thought I had dealt with "God"!

Do not concentrate on the high-colored (and rather delightful) stylization of Zen. Beneath that there is serious "work" done.

As regards "experiences," Bucke mentions many of course. That type may have differing results. One person may guard it as a jealous secret all his or her life and as the most wonderful thing. On the other hand Sir Julian Huxley, who is a high-type "humanist," may have several such experiences and regard them as purely subjective. They are not rare. They are "valid" (not subjective), but having one does not enable one to prove their validity. Sir Julian Huxley is an obvious case in point. They can come to anyone.

They are discussed fairly often, but there seems almost a conspiracy of silence about the "understanding" we are dealing with in these letters because for one thing it is quite rare, and for another, the words, "an experience," do not properly describe such a fundamental revelation and discovery. Have you read what the Upanishads, for example, say about it?

I am not "threatening to drop your case," but am rather aware that you do not even show verbal desire for this thing — and many do. Further, you must believe that without any desire to press this upon you,

I am actuated only by consideration for you—because life can be rough. If there is nothing in you that wants it, you cannot blame me for the obvious realization that we would not get anywhere, except to recrimination—and that is undesirable.

All through the ages misguided followers of "awakened" men, filled with zeal, have endeavored by assertions of miracles and marvels to boost their master's reputation, whereas such things are quite beside the point.

Zen says that to desire miracles is to try to put another head over your own. In plain English, the marvel is to be found in what we are already familiar with—writing a letter or drinking a glass of water—in the so-called "commonplace."

Naturally I want your photograph—is that such a terrible request? Did I send you mine? If not I will at once do so. Or is there some special reason, as was the case with a lady student of mine who was terribly disfigured in an accident?

Friendship is desirable in a study of this type because the delicate discrimination required is not attainable in an atmosphere of cynical distrust, picayune carping and falsetto accusations. Even a psychical researcher gets further if he approaches this often murky subject in a pleasant manner. But leave this matter for the moment.

The experiences you mention come unasked and unexpected. They leave the ego the same as before, <u>almost</u>.

The understanding we are dealing with demands an abnegation of ego—<u>even if only once, yet completely</u>. (You will find this exemplified in the remarks of every sage through the ages—for instance, Heraclitus, Gautama, Lao Tse—all around 500 BC when there was such an abrupt change from the

evolved animistic and sacrificial cults, as dealt with by
Fraser and other anthropologists.)

This is for us humans usually a real problem.
For me it was nearly impossible. The friend who is
assisting you (as a sort of catalyst) does not have a
pleasant job because ego starts a furious battle by any
and every method—tricky, snide, violent,
withdrawing and so forth. (The same is true in
psychotherapy, but it is diluted so that the ego doesn't
get so inflamed. It is "diluted" because the "attack" on
ego is slow, long drawn-out, gradual, gentle—and
highly profitable!)

You will never while you live find any other
"way," since intellect alone cannot do the job and only
revolves in its own squirrel-cage. You will never find a
teacher-friend who will let you fix the conditions of
"work," because then you are using your ego to work
on ego and that is self-defeating.

This is how it is. I cannot change it. It is an
"odd" universe you and I are born in and will die in.

Friend,
Alfred

October 31

Dear Richard,

<u>Brain-washing or brain-sucking</u>? I am not a "movement" and I haven't "sucked the brain-blood of mankind." Very few people write to me, and those that "succeed" (even those that do not) are not less intelligent but more so, not less skeptical but more so. My line is not belief—it is proof. However, there is a paradox (if there were not the whole world would be "awakened"!): The first step must be belief that proof will come.

Like many others I wondered what satori was, what the Oriental religions were all about, what Gautama, Eckhart, Lao Tse, Jesus, Heraclitus, etc. experienced. I soon found that there was <u>something</u>, and to little Alfred that was a sufficient challenge. But one has first to dip one toe in the ocean.

<u>Sense or no-sense</u>? But speaking of "brain-blood" and so forth, you negate your own early words (Aug 17), "I have come to look upon reason as the vanity of the intellect." The truth is you are still the Supreme Court to yourself, even though Heraclitus says: "One should extinguish hubris more carefully than a great conflagration—and not leave a spark." (Hubris = pride, presumption.)

What do you hope to find—and <u>where</u>? Answer me. You know, and your letters show it, that there is absolutely no way to gain anything by a verbal understanding. If one could, then let us publish it right away in the magazines and newspapers! By "anything" I mean "anything ultimate," as regards ourselves and this universe—the source of it, or what is responsible for it.

Thus there is only one way left. It is work on

oneself, and it is found—since you cannot decide not to decide, which is essential—that a friend or teacher is necessary.

If I were "only a searcher for truth" we could go on yak-yakking our fool heads off and the correspondence would really be piddling—as piddling as philosophy or art-criticism. As Lao Tse says, "Flat, no obvious goal."

Whether I were working personally with you or by mail (as so few, if any, do), the kind of work would be the same, seemingly "flat, stale and unprofitable," distasteful, uninteresting, no new discoveries, no tid-bits, no theories, plodding, annoying, with no obvious aim or goal, and no obvious *raison d'être* (reason for being).

Why is this? A smart fellow would see at once. I have a well-stocked library, and I could (and have done so) write fascinating stuff, like, say, Manly Palmer Hall in his "Horizon" magazine. There you can get the low-down, inside stuff on Nostradamus, The Tarot, The Hung Society, Diana of the Ephesians, The Kundalini, Dante, Blake, Mandala Magic, The Harmon Papers, The Nuremberg Chronicle, The Tribes in the Light Blue Mountains, and so forth.

Beware when the self is pleased! Ego purrs. This is the life. Ego is pleased. But that is the whole trouble. These glamorous things actually leave a worse taste behind. It is like knowing how the illusionists and professional magicians do their tricks. It gets terribly blah!

There is One Self, not many. You hold it away by your insistence (like most people) in holding to the hegemony (predominance) of your "self." When your hand finally releases its hold of the bedclothes, your pretended "ownership" of your body (which you do not even "run"), and of your consciousness (as though it were a piece of real estate), ceases—but the Consciousness goes on. What will happen to you will happen to me.

However, you can know the One Self-Consciousness as well as you know anyone—indeed far better. By "know" I mean really know, know by experience, know by acquaintance, know intimately—not any of the theological hot-air and clap-trap. I speak as a mathematician with accounting and auditing background and scientific education—not as a dweller on cloud 51 or a "true believer."

Ego kicks up! You are judging all the time: "I am impatient," (lucky I am not), "I feel it is a dog chasing its tail—a strange ritual." You are like all the rest—maybe more inaccessible.

You said, "A strange and fruitful ritual," as a bare possibility. Well, I have been successful with several friends, and they did "attain," and they did say, "How could you have put up with this nonsense?" (just exactly like yours), and I said, "My teacher put up with me."

When you stop trying to run the show and to discover some verbalized magic, when the maturing change starts to show in self-indulgent and smart-aleck Richard, then I know we are on the way. As yet you have merely fenced, and shown no participation or understanding. Heraclitus said, "Dogs bark at what they do not understand." So while I chase my tail you bark! (But I am not implying you are a dog or even an s.o.b.)

I am not a psychoanalyst. You are fully capable of tracing your own attitude to various childish manifestations, if that is the cause. "I don't wanna, Mom. I don't wanna," and he grows up another C.G. Jung. Boy, oh boy. But be comforted. Suzuki said of me, "No hope and not worth the effort." He was right, it was impossible. But it happened—because to the One, nothing is "impossible." So if it happened to Alfred, who was worse (if possible!) than you, it could happen to you.

Friend,
Alfred

November 14

Dear Richard,

Forget about me (for the sake of argument) for the moment. Take a Zen master. Sokatsu Shaku on his seventieth birthday (April 16, 1939) said that in his 40 years of teaching 3000 men and women came to study Zen. In the 40 years only 13 completed the training and of these only 4 became teachers in turn. These 4 were Zuizan Goto, Eisan Tatsuta, Chikudo Ghasama and Sokei-An (who "worked" in New York and founded "The First Zen Institute," which still exists — the Zen Master there now is Miura Roshi).

These 4 men were remarkable men. I know several persons who knew Sokei-An. (See "Cat's Yawn," fairly easily obtainable — a reprint of issues of a magazine published by and written by Sokei-An). As for Chikudo Ghasama (who studied also at Heidelberg), a friend of mine (an "awakened" man) "worked" in Berlin with Ghasama.

"<u>Proof</u>"? Now! What "proof" could any of these Zen Masters give you? What would you accept as "proof"? If Jesus called on you one day, what would you require as "proof"? If two spies met in Nazi Germany and each told the other they were working for the Allies, what proof could they give one another? All documents would mean nothing. How could they get together? What proof could anyone give of something that was a personal experience?

After Jesus was supposed to feed 5000 with 5 loaves of bread and 2 fishes, the religious leaders asked him for a "sign." Wow! What did they want? More? Red, white and blue rays from every pore, like poor Gautama?? It is not a matter of "ignorance" and "authority." I am imposing nothing on you, and

71

expect nothing of you. But you wrote me, and I have no earthly way of knowing what you desire as proof. You never tell me. The "Supreme Court" has established clear rules of evidence, and in law what is admissible and what is not admissible is clearly codified.

"<u>Said</u>"? But you wait to hear anything whatever that is <u>said</u>, and automatically (and correctly) reply "nyet" (no)! "Doubt" in you is more than skepticism. It is a "quest."

"<u>Done</u>"? Then if you see something <u>done</u>, what is that to you? Is that what you want? Miracles? Wonders? "Signs"? A little levitation? One of my letters appearing under your plate without coming through the mails? A vision? What? What would you regard as "proof"?

Please include a stamped addressed envelope. A mere psychotherapist who talks to you for 5 years (or you to him) may cost $6,500 or more (say $25 a week). So a .04 stamp is still cheap — and I don't get it as revenue. Uncle Sam gets it. If it isn't worth that to you, then the thing for you to do is obvious. But have the decency to write a pleasant last letter and say good-bye like a human being.

Friend,
Alfred

Dear Richard,

Your question is eminently "reasonable." What is to be done if you meet a Zen master (says the koan)? Shall you talk to him, ignore him or sock him on the chin?

<u>Another attitude</u>: Sometimes a student will say: "I give in. I am through trying to argue. I am at your disposal." What do we do then? Contact God and have him send a wheelbarrow to collect the student?

<u>Student has to do it himself</u>: Alas! Even the saints of old wrestled with themselves for years in the desert, as did Gautama the "Buddha." But the student wants supreme satisfaction, supreme enlightenment, health, the equivalent of a $5000 psychologist etc. — all for a casual grudging word and a "might as well, it don't cost nothing" attitude.

<u>Your attitude</u>: This however is not yet your position. You are demonstrating to me graphically that one cannot "decide, or decide not to decide," or "write without demonstrating conceit or a pretense at reason." That is, you are not saying, "I am convinced that there is something to attain. How do we attain it?" Oh no! You are just making a point. If you were "convinced" there would be much to say — in particular how you had changed from the letters before when you had all your intellectual spines up like a porcupine and your dichotomizing "reason" all agog to tear everything in half. Then we could go on from there.

<u>I'll show him.</u> But your letter is merely a device in the arguments you put up (valid or not it doesn't matter) in the pushing away of something you don't

especially want. Better bring on the dancing girls to stir your jaded appetite. It won't be until the years start coming alarmingly quickly, perhaps, that you will awake from your leaden lethargy.

Then we are "at home." This is not "blame" of course. No ethics are involved here. If for some reason the time is not ripe (and I do not know all the conditions that make one agog for "awakening"), then there are satisfactions in life to be had. "Unnumbered ways of dream," as the poet says.

Half an hour a day? Not that! And after all, how much in any day are most persons actually even "conscious"? Only when it becomes necessary to make a decision! Thus a person could be fully aware and awake from 8 - 8.03 am, 12 - 12.05 pm, 7 - 7.05 pm etc. — and could wear a sign, "Open for business as follows: ----"

A test. Ouspensky says you could be walking down the street and could say to yourself, "I must remember myself." Then you would go on, "I know I see a taxi passing. I know a man and a woman are going by. I see the building across the street. I know..." and all of a sudden it is three hours later and you say, "My goodness. I forgot to remember myself!" We are prisoners of our day-dreaming. And so life goes by.

Note however. (But you will realize this is not the "awakening" I refer to. That is not voluntary — even though one "works" toward it.) I was merely sketching a way of life, the usual one. There is a Mentor book "The Teachings of the Mystics," by Walter T. Stace, and although he is only a philosopher, and mixes up "mystical experiences" with "awakening," nevertheless it might help to establish the mere existence of that which I speak and which I claim to know myself and to have assisted others to.

74

<u>Back to the problem</u>. I find it quite possible to write "awakened" friends! It is perhaps necessary to be genuinely "open" and not snide or tricky, but to be just naturally friendly. There is no reason to avoid "reason," especially when it is keen "discrimination."

<u>One occasion only</u>! As for "egotism" and "conceit," those are our birthrights—yours and mine, but once, just <u>once</u>, and *really truly,* they must be shed. After that you can resume—but it won't be quite the same!

Friend,
Alfred

February 20, 1961

Dear Richard,

"<u>Fleeced by a cult</u>." Thanks for the analogy! "They reduced the aspirant to wordlessness by attacking everything he said."

It happened to my teacher, but she "happened" to be at the point where this was the decisive factor. Hence, me! Hence, your letter to me!

But suppose the aspirant says (to himself), "I will go and have lunch and a glass of wine with my girl friend, and listen to Saint-Saens Violin Concerto No. 3, or Tschaikovsky Piano Concerto No. 2, or Scriabin's (only) Piano Concerto, or Dvorak's 'Four Romantic Pieces,' or something of Paganini or a later Beethoven quartet"?

What is he "saying" in all this? Nothing, only experiencing. Suppose it was the other way: "They tempted the aspirant to unending loquacity by judicious praise and the introduction of exciting and controversial topics"? What was done? What was decided? Who cares now?

"<u>I conclude you to be either a liar or a well-nigh incomprehensible man since you do not appear to be deranged</u>." (Oh boy! How rude I could get to little Richard! But down Fido!) The point is, of course, that you are still using "comprehend" or "understand" intellectually. Actually to you I am not "well-nigh" but "completely" incomprehensible, and it is this we must face and conquer as it has always been conquered. Luke 18:27 "Who then can be saved (metanoia = "changed")?"

"<u>Are there any who become immortal?</u>" Unclear. All "bodies" decay some day (my self-important friend) , unless you believe Elijah, Enoch,

Mary and Jesus "ascended" taking their body with them. Does "immortal" mean "last for unending time"? If that is what you mean then your mind (which is responsible for putting a time sequence into events) must survive unendingly. Since I have not (a) contacted any dead relatives or friends, nor (b) lived until the year infinity AD, which is a long way away yet, it would be unscientific of me to answer you.

Maybe in 19,610,000,000,000,000,000 AD, Richard, now reduced only to his mind, will say to me (in a similar position), "Do you remember our discussions?" Except that he will not say it with his lips, because those have decayed long ago. No doubt you will say, "In all this long time I have pretty well exhausted Richard's repertoire of half-baked scientific facts, pornographic and sadistic imaginings (annoying when the organ has gone the way of all flesh), smart rejoinders, convoluted conjectures, wishful thinking, childhood and baby memories..." and who knows, perhaps even one or two loving and altruistic wishes that didn't quite reach action. "Well, here I am, Richard, still me, more bored with 'me' than ever in the 19,609,999,999,999,999,980 years since my death.

But still hanging on, still full of fight, and only infinity minus 19,609,999,999,999,999,980 years to go. That's a cinch. Infinity here I come!"

"Is it just the knowledge of our nothingness?" Just the opposite.

"What are your plans for the future?" No plans while Richard is arsing about in the preliminary stages with spurts of correspondence. When Richard is nearly ready to dip one toe in the ocean, I will then tell him what to do.

"If you wish I can visit you." Well I have a nice place here (on 12 acres) but since neither my wife nor I are young we find entertaining a chore, except in the case of close, congenial friends—and frankly, right now, you would be a pain in the neck.

There is much delight here. There are 3 artists, my wife, my teacher and myself—in 3 houses, 2 close and 1 half a mile away. I can "work" as well by mail as personally (better), so do not need to make this a place of residence for students as I once contemplated. All this is purely friendly, and no question of money or gifts ever arises—what we are dealing with transcends such things.

When you are a bit "housebroken," so to say— if ever you get that far (and you are only hanging on by your eyebrows now)—then you and I can meet and chuckle over the long and bumpy road. (Sometimes a short road, but always bumpy.) I am willing to be "friends," but that word means an awful lot. Friends trust one another, would share all they have, would even trust their lives to one another. That is a long way.

Right now your approach to me is as follows: Another cultist? A liar? Incomprehensible? May have to be placated? Must know a lot more about him. A guesser. One who doesn't define God. Maybe well-meaning. One who "should" know whether he has had past lives. One who "should" be able to push Richard over. One who "should" be meek and good-tempered (confusing me with "religionists"), and meekly present his rear-end for Richard's little boot.

"I presume that he who knows God knows everything." When (If!) you "work" with me, you had better stop "presuming" so much and get scientific. Experience shows that you are wrong. The process is to unlearn not to "learn," and finally you finish up "knowing" nothing.

Of course I "know" as much at least as you, having read much, studied at college and elsewhere, and all that. Indeed, you may not have had your esthetic side very well developed, as I see nothing in your letters but a constant repetition of, "How can I know the unknowable?" plus a little primitive mind-discussion not even deserving to be called psychology, and much misconception of a quasi-magical nature about past lives, immortal bodies and what not. *Alla podrida* [an incongruous mixture or miscellaneous collection].

Immortality and the beatific vision for .04 cents, says my wife. Well, why not? One fellow said, "Light a fire under me." So I did. And one day he said, "Consciousness sees itself! It is impossible, yet it happens." So I knew. And others one by one came along with their characteristic phrases.

But if I told Richard all these things he would have (a) a collection of phrases to flumdoodle someone, and (b) a collection of testimonials. Always there have been none ("testimonials").

Always the student was told, "Follow me." "Why?" "No reason." "Yes." And that's that. But you can consult the tremendous literature of the Orient on *jivan-muktis* in Hinduism, liberated persons in Buddhism, adepts in classical Taoism, masters in Zen and so forth. In Christianity there was Eckhart and many others. There was Gautama, Jesus, Lao Tse, Bapak Subuh, etc., and they knew "something" too.

Is this all the "flimsy" and "nonsensical," "mythological" side of the race's progress? Did consciousness emerge at a stage of matter's evolution—and mind too?

The musicians seemed to know "something" (some of them), and some poets. Why do people shy away from this if they merely regard it as trivial? To them it is not trivial, but to be feared (as ego destructive).

"Shall I give you honesty while you toy with evasiveness? To "toy with evasiveness" implies a degree of conscious deception. Now this might be some technique of "working," and so I might be entitled to it in view of the greater good. However, I have not done any such thing, and the trouble lies in the fact that there is indeed no way whatever of "conveying" the experience.

A good thing! Why? Because anything "explainable" would be liable to counterattack in words, and fortunately this is "experience" (as real as a color or a sound), and so stands on its own feet and is not verbalizable.

I am not "trying to verbalize something." The meter I observe (around 2 o'clock for you) is not "degree of understanding or learning" but something between the lines—which is my real concern. Until that meter goes round to nearly 12 o'clock, the rule is for you to keep talking, even recite, "Mary had a little lamb," and in letters, keep writing, since blank sheets of paper are not enough.

My words "housebroken" and so forth are not mere abuse, but if you will observe, refer to fundamental changes in a person—maturity, softening up, humanity, etc. Take an underprivileged kid and try to explain why he mustn't spit on the carpet, and at first he will say, "What the hell does it matter?" Later things may seem different—but so will the kid be.

And if you don't change, then look out! Something there is that plays rough.

"I waited awhile to see if you were doing something for effect (shocks and gimmicks as in Zen." Such kind cooperation should be appreciated—but I don't. The surgeon has the advantage of an unconscious patient. I want a natural one, not two

80

beady eyes looking out for "techniques" — which they won't find!

"<u>What would you have me do? I cannot decide not to decide.</u>" Well then, "not decide to not decide." (Boils down to eventual spontaneity, sincerity. Nothing less will do.)

Just before critical moments in our lives we may be favored either with a clear intimation of what to do, or even by a flash of the "real state of affairs" (as I maintain, naturally, not you).

Abraham Lincoln, on April 13, 1865, had a quasi-dream in which he saw that individuality was a mere difference in brain-folds. An identical force was speaking through Grant, Lincoln, Jefferson Davis, Robert E. Lee and old John Brown. A mighty, conscious, creative entity, as subtle and all pervasive as electricity, but possessed of every capacity men's souls and minds possessed — an entity which manifested itself through all forms of life. If so, why? To what end?

If the law of heredity produced Jeff Davis and Lincoln and a slave trader, did it mean that the force deliberately limited — by a good or bad or inadequate brain — its own spiritual expression?

By the eternal verities, it looked as if this were true. It looked as if existence were a stupendously earnest game in which the creator had set himself the task of bringing all life to vivid consciousness of its complete identity with him. And when, as the aeons rolled, man became completely conscious that his soul and the creator's were one and the same... Lincoln covered his eyes with his hand.

This call, heard with his spiritual ear, what was it but the wakening knowledge that he was not Abraham Lincoln — save for this moment of existence? Actually, he was one with all life, forever. The call, did it not mean that that larger segment of himself—which dwelt far, far beyond the outposts of human thought—was putting itself in communion with that infinitesimal segment known as Abraham Lincoln, telling Lincoln that all was well.

And with an increasing wonder he realized that for the first time since conscious thought began with him, he was not lonely. Never to be lonely again! That which was imprisoned in the poor frame of Abraham Lincoln had envisaged its real identity, had sighted its true home.

Happiness! This, then was happiness! Its other name was God. (From "Great Captain," Honoré Morrow)

Next day he was assassinated. But he had told his wife, had told Stanton. Is it happiness or a bitter-sweet joy? What words can we choose? (The bitterness of maturity, the sweetness of a child.) Words refer to things we have known. Here is something comparable to…   What words for such a change? "Animal becoming a man?" says Richard, "How wild can your comparisons get?"

Let us see. Experiments have shown that to a certain age animals outstrip human children. But children develop self-consciousness—and that is an overwhelming change. Do they learn this, study to do this? No. Not formally, anyway. But they learn a language, and that is a powerful weapon fashioned by self-conscious people full of such concepts—even the words "self-conscious." Further, they observe and copy available adults. One day the world is seen with new eyes and the child may think it has a unique faculty. This is soon corrected by experience.

It would seem to be easier to take the next step, to <u>S</u>elf <u>C</u>onsciousness. We have a language skill. We have some feeling of "self." It is true that until it occurs to us we can not know it. But it was the same with self-consciousness, and besides, there are a number of people who assure us it happened to them, and that it is an "experience," or rather a sudden change in consciousness (like "seeing a joke," perhaps).

But we jib. We say it is a false analogy, there is no such thing, it does not happen. But we cover ourselves by adding, "If something happens it means nothing and is of no importance."

Our friends who are "awakened" say, "Since you have little to lose except a few minutes now and then, and everything to gain—truly 'Everything'—then isn't it a good gamble?" But we really fear to go on with this, and so we just go on arguing.

First we say, "What are the techniques?" Well, in a way the same as for "self-consciousness," i.e. using the language and observation of the guru (who is "adult" compared with you). But there is obviously more than that. We must exceed the "self" concept, not remove it, because it is the essence of a human-being. But we must surrender it so that the Self can come in. This we cannot usually do by ourselves.

Consider the other side of the question. The guru is willing to give all his time and best efforts to help the student without hope of reward or even thanks. He expects every kind of ingratitude, slippery business and gray hairs. He expects the student to argue indefinitely, even though that produces no experiences. He finds the student wants to direct the procedure to some extent, to know all the methods, what is being done and so forth (even if it makes it impossible to help him to realization!). He finds the student is just an "Indian-receiver," criticizing everything in great detail and wanting everything done as comfortably as possible, until finally his guru gently takes him in a plush-lined wheelbarrow and dumps him in the Seventh Heaven—which he goggles at with a furred tongue and a lackadaisical eye. Or perhaps he has a push-button mechanism installed.

After all, with so many advertisers and sects competing for him, should he not get a bit choosy? The guru is sympathetic and not sadistic by nature. Indeed, he knows what is going on (and alas—what will go on) and so he does his best.

But the One stays away. You can fool the guru (perhaps), bully the guru, placate the guru, bamboozle him—but apparently not the One Self. Oh well, very annoying, try again. ("How does the One penetrate my insincerity?" Not too difficult is it?)

"I will not overlook with haste anyone who claims (Caution observable! Whatever will become of you?) to be able to attain—no, to have attained—this knowledge."

Friend,
Alfred

P.S. Sometimes the student plays a game, like those geniuses who cannot look after themselves. So, for the sake of their genius, a bunch of people (maybe several women) must feed them, clothe them, console them, get them out of scrapes, look after their health and so on in face of all discouragements—even in face of blank, ignorant ingratitude. So the student says, "I disbelieve you and everything, but it is your job to save me. Go ahead!" But there is a catch in this—something the student doesn't realize.

Dear Richard,

Evaluation: This continues while the Universe awaits your decision! Naturally you will soon repeat yourself. I do not know what data would satisfy you. Metaphysical discussion is useless yet we keep bringing up such questions as "merger with the One" or "eternal life of the mind" that cannot be answered verbally and require "experience." (Incidentally I did not say the mind lives unendingly. What does go on, or better, what does not cease, is better known by this same personal experience.)

"Hiding behind the postage stamp." There is nothing "odd" or harmful here, although your word "unusual" has some truth in it. Sometimes I am sad (for people like yourself), but always compassionate. I have not gotten "big," as you suggest. What I have is in all of us. Those who seem famous, like St. Germain, Cagliostro, might not be of much use to you when you get behind the showmanship. Simple, unassuming people may be the true "knowers."

As for "what is a guru?" a teacher does not actually "teach" anything, but quietly persists like a mother until the child grows up, with often no thanks and asking no reward.

Kriya yoga: There is confusion here. Patanjali uses this as "preliminary" yoga, but Yogananda made it his main technique. In any case, it stresses "union," which means there are two things yet to be joined. It is the other way round! The One thing exists, and there is already "union." But you will not lose yourself in it, nor your self-consciousness, while you live. Words are of no help here.

Transcendentalists? We paint pictures, play the

recorder, toboggan down the hill, but have no need to use silly words like "transcendentalists." You are having nightmares. Such talk is for those who have not "attained" and have not started to live. Does such talk help you at all?

All knowledge? To answer a host of your questions, I am no more learned than "before," cannot levitate or do miracles, cannot speak with the dead — in fact only a close friend could see any difference at all.

"There is a light in my eye you might not like." I didn't notice it. But you can always retire in a cloud of recriminations and say, "These fakers don't get very far with me." I have known this done before and it gives satisfaction, no doubt, to the person who does it (at least for a time).

As for me, "The Lord gives and the Lord takes away." One comes, one goes. Or else you could "search" forever — for searching's sake — with (paradoxically!) no thought of "finding." Some fear to find.

I shall give you no testimonials, however (those are confidential), nor paint glowing pictures of attainment or threats if you don't, nor promise marvels and magic. (The beautiful thing in the world is the order, not the leeway — which does exist.) Nor can I "beg" too much, as this thing may not be debauched or debased, and it would be undignified and twist our relations round. Usually the student seeks the guru then does as he is told. How else can we tame ego?

Summary: There is a remarkable disproportion between the low tone of our correspondence (bathrooms and plumbing are our top levels) and the drastic and final change in a person that should be our real theme. This "awakening" is for the childlike, the simple at heart, but not necessarily for those either lacking in keen discrimination or in natural culture. "Wise as serpents, innocent as doves."

Nor is this work usually undertaken in a trivial, calculating way. It is the most important thing that can happen to any human being, and appears to be the specific reason for the existence of the universe. Lincoln discovered this on April 13, 1865.

Friend,
Alfred

Dear Richard,

"Conversational fodder" is apparently the best we can hope for yet. Actually a paucity of language such as yours does not reflect a difficulty of finding something to say, but rather shows a very high degree of selectivity among your no-doubt very numerous thoughts. You hand out to me the fewest possible scraps, conveying the fewest possible indications as to you yourself. If I were a psychoanalyst (and I certainly am not) getting $25 or $30 per hour for your revelations, I think you might eventually feel that more cooperation would mean more money's worth. Yet no doubt many patients lie mum on the much publicized couch session after session. To hell with economy!

If two people getting married asked, "What shall we talk about?" I should notify any lawyer friend I had who handles divorce work to keep an eye on them!

Normally the procedure toward "awakening" goes something like this:

<u>Stage 1</u>: Battered by the storms of life or driven by an interior compulsion — or even some "experience" — a person becomes dissatisfied with his or her current religion (or the lack of it), and drifts and studies such things as Unity, Theosophy, Christian Science, Rosicrucianism, Zen, etc. Possibly they will read Huxley's "Perennial Philosophy" and dip into the Far Eastern texts now so easily available. They may get the idea that there is a thing called liberation or awakening or satori or realization, although it seems extremely vague and their passion for miracles and marvels gets mixed up with it.

Stage 2: Sooner or later the "master" or "guru" idea comes up, since the student gets nowhere by himself or herself usually. To "pick" a master or guru cold turkey is not at all easy because there are not enough available for picking and choosing. However, there are the correspondence courses, the Essene Society, the Brotherhood of Light, etc. (I make up names, although I may have guessed an actual name—it does not matter.)

I often wonder whether some of these are not genuine and could actually do the job. However, the attention one gets needs to be far more individualized and personal because this is not "learning." It is partly a <u>transmission through friendship or love</u>. One does not usually sell these things.

Then there are the Swamis of the Vedanta Society—very well educated and high-toned men indeed, and they conduct yoga classes. There is a Zen master in New York at the First Zen Institute. Here we touch more satisfactory gurus. The question of "how long" each of these takes is to be considered, and of course these do <u>not</u> "work" by mail. Is there any genuine guru who does?

The student may meet by good luck (if that is the proper word) a master, such as a rare one in the Taoist succession or some other kind. (There are people in USA belonging to no sect, cult or religion, who "work" as I do, suiting my vocabulary to the student's habits. Again, few work by mail, if any.)

The student by now is getting a good idea (even though he is not "awakened") of what he wants and how to judge. Remember, I am speaking of personal interviews. He may drift from guru to guru (all good) until he reaches one that really suits him.

Meanwhile it is assumed that the student has gradually become more and more familiar with the

"Perennial Philosophy" or "Wisdom Religion" (or whatever term you use to describe what Honoré Morrow puts into the mouth and mind of her character Lincoln).

It becomes clear that "awakening" consists of realizing that we have come from and return to this One Self (to speak crudely perhaps). At this stage the student is said to "dip one toe in the ocean," i.e. to accept the general theory or doctrine and be ready to accept "work."

<u>Stage 3</u>: I do not wish to go into the whole technique of work with a guru, but one thing is clear. The student realizes that "awakening" or "realization" will never come unless at least once the student has surrendered the "boss-concept" of ego or self—the idea that it is a Supreme Court in itself, self-sufficient, "Captain of My Soul" (as Henley boasts and poor Bertrand Russell squeaks after him). Since the student is seeking to realize "that" to which he is subordinate, second-in-command, it is obvious he must lower his flag and admit his lower status at some point.

It is extremely easy for one person, even like you, to hold the great "God" (so-called) of the Universe <u>away</u>. One little finger suffices. Even a penny can hide the sun. Thus without your active cooperation, and agreement to do as your guru says, there is not even a ghost of a chance of realization. If the student wishes to "win," he should not be a student because it is hard enough when both guru and student are eagerly cooperating! Such a "win" is a Pyrrhic victory—it is far too easy.

Thus in Japan the applicant must wait outside the gates of the monastery a day or so. It is done rather symbolically now. Once it was very real and the applicant was repulsed, treated roughly, told to go away and the gate slammed in his face. But nowadays

90

with Ipana toothpaste with Hexa-Hexachlorophene and innumerable detergents competing over TV, little Richard wants to be wooed, gently persuaded, urged to enter. The $1,000,000 bill must be washed and ironed and handed over on a silken cushion before he will accept it.

<u>Technical summary</u>: However you are not in Stage 3, of course. You are not even in Stage 1 since you have no active interest, apparently, in the subject under discussion, and throw down a couple of languid lines (like a bone for the dog) to keep our dragging correspondence going for a few more staggering steps (like a drunk collapsing against a friendly lamp post).

Fortunately, some have said to me, "Light a Fire under me." Some have said, "My daughter says my face has changed." And so on and so on. But I will give you no testimonials or references. You will have to make your own decision (and <u>pretty soon</u>, because this letter is completely explanatory of the whole position).

A man once asked, "How much is this yacht?" The salesman said "If you ask that you should not have one!" So, how will you know your guru? If you ask that, you will never know—in fact the whole subject is not very pressing to you now. (If he hesitates, however, sell him to a side-show.)

<u>Answers</u>: Is the "word" of God an audible sound? Some people have strong visualizing abilities. Some can "imagine" sounds very well. Some go further and have hallucinations or delusions. These are interesting faculties and can even be annoying if excessive. They are dealt with in numerous books and articles everywhere, as in "Search" up to "To Morrow." "Search" dealt with such "sounds" recently. If you are not telling me that you have such "voices"

91

why not tell me straightforwardly?

However, "awakening" or satori or realization of God is like seeing a joke, or jumping to an explanation, and nothing involving the senses occurs at that time—at least not in the way you mean! Since realization is, among other things, increased sanity (health of body and mind), colors may get sharper, appreciation of beauty in Nature and Art more intense, health may improve. One may even "see" (but not with the eyes, really) how the One shines through the Many, but this I will not discuss, as it will confuse the issue.

Thus nobody "sees" God or "talks" with God in the normal sense of those words, unless it is something that has not come to my attention (and anything can happen it seems). Open up and be frank please.

<u>Answers</u> (cont.): Why is it "important to spread the knowledge of oblivion"? It may not be oblivion, as you say, but those who surrender the boss-concept of ego may have experiences in which ego desires nothing so much as to <u>exit</u>.

The average person who happens to get a horror of revolving his few memories for 1,000,000,000,000,000,000,000,000,000 years (then realizes he hasn't made a dent in unending time) and seeks an <u>exit</u> may be frustrated, since to kill the body or commit suicide, according to current beliefs, only starts him off on the wrong foot in the next world. Thus, 1,000,000,000,000,000,000,000,000,000 years might as well start as happily as possible!

The Theosophists hold out "rebirth" in other lives as a prize. The Orientals regard it as a curse, as being "bound to the wheel." Those who "know God" are eager to find the way back, to find the way home. This particular personality compared to that "open," lovely Thing is seen as dreadful indeed.

But to "wake up" to God is <u>not</u> oblivion. When your dream-self "wakes up" in the morning you have not ever spared one thought for your poor dream self! It reached "oblivion" when you woke up. So what do you do? You break your breakfast egg, toast your bread and laugh at your dream adventures. Quite heartless, you see!

Do you think you could be a little more human and a trifle less verbally constipated? Letters such as you have so far favored me with are not promising. I have explained why. It is not for me to "play God," but if you can get anywhere by such tactics then I am a monkey's uncle!

Friend,
Alfred

Dear Richard,

Long discourse on "analysis. Yes, I suppose I must be careful in any reference to "psychotherapy." There is a book recently published called the "Frog Pond," I believe, that gives a lady's experiences with 6 psychoanalysts. One she calls "Silent Simon." He used to listen and say nothing at all, but take notes. On Thursday he saw a friend who told him what to say on Friday!

I think your observations are very sound and, as you say, the "normal" doesn't mean much. You never remove your "aberrations" but you do learn to live with them or to supersede them, "go above them." After three years and $5,000 there ought to be some results! But often it goes on indefinitely.

Further, the analyst may be pretty aberrated and bad-tempered himself, and a very confused man. They vary of course, and there might be a rare one or two (as in the "Frog Pond," the last two analysts) who has a gift for the job and who makes an art of it. However, there are few of them and millions of people in mental trouble.

One thing everybody needs is "love" (in the correct sense — outgoing friendship, asking nothing except to help). Doctors call it TLC (tender, loving care). Many women would therefore be far more capable of helping the mentally troubled, but in our society men predominate in most professions.

I regard the method of digging up item by item from the unconscious or subconscious remunerative ($$$) for the analyst, but a long, long way round — the "analytical" instead of the "synthetical." Let me explain. I had a friend who was forced to study singing by his mother and he did not like it as a child. In retrospect my friend could always "bring up" from the past a flood of tears and no doubt could do this for ever. This was not the way to help him. However, merely by speaking very frankly and naturally to him as a friend, he snapped right out of it and today is a highly successful man.

The Freudian analysts have just a few standard "complexes" (incestual love for mother, hatred of father, fear of castration, etc.) which everybody is supposed to be deeply affected by. The patient always "brings up" this material (not without help and "direction," I'm sure).

The Jungians have their own standard set of "archetypes," and these too the student or patient faithfully "brings up" (with a little help, I think!). I have seen the same person do this with a Freudian and Jungian analyst respectively. It is a joke. No doubt the Adlerians would find the "inferiority complex" to be the real source of trouble. If, then, I advise the "synthetical," what do I mean? Well, the truth is I only chose that word as a contrast to "analytic," but what I mean is some overall method that does not need this searching for infinite detail.

Actually, it is found in the course of "work" for awakening that the student becomes what is called "normal" (socially acceptable?) in a very short time. It is even true that it is easier for a very aberrated (or slightly psychotic) person to jump to "awakening" (which is severe sanity) much faster than a so-called "normal" person who is full of "controls." Why is this? It is because awakening-therapy is directed <u>contra ego</u>. That is, not to remove ego—which is absurd poppycock since consciousness includes self-consciousness, and unless you kill someone or make them unconscious "ego" or "self" is still there. <u>It is</u>

"us" <u>while we live</u>, of course.

Nevertheless, there is a disease of ego and it is the idea that <u>we</u> are the final authority! It is a surprising thing. We are born into a wonderful but puzzling world. We never solve the problems of what we are and where we are, nor why we are, but we keep going from one "solution" to another (hopefully), and always with the idea that we are the judge, the decider, the Supreme Court, the Court of Last Resort. It takes smashing blows of adversity, death, illness, unhappiness to undermine our cockiness, and even from the fire there is a last feeble cry of proud self-assertion. Odd.

It is not for everybody. Some are born with a touch of aspiration for a deep beauty and understanding as shown in music, Nature, the Arts, Love, etc.—which involves surrender of the smart-aleck self, throwing oneself into <u>experience</u> rather than reaching it by any logical or reasoning process. These people are smart because they realize naturally that <u>anything</u> that can be thought and then said (or written or printed) can be controverted by other thoughts and words. There is <u>no finality in words</u>.

"Science" is a way of winning difficult knowledge of how Nature works, but of course cannot answer questions like "what" is so and so. Each discovery merely needs one more, and so on forever. I wonder if there is one scientist anywhere who is so foolish as to imagine that the ultimate nature of things and ourselves will ever be reached by physics and psychology, respectively.

As a matter of fact, "psychology" deals with everything <u>but</u> the nature of the mind itself. Facing this dilemma, it is welcome news that there is a way to break through. The experience so obtained is personal and can be passed only to a few. Yet "millions" of people follow the Buddha's remarks and call it a "religion." In the case of Christianity we call it "God."

People say to me, "Oh, your work is religious. It is to find God." I agree with them to avoid semantics, but isn't it obvious that this puts the cart before the horse?! The "experience" is primary, and at this stage there are no names, no descriptions. If some idiots want to make something (a new religion!) out of my remarks they can, but it will not mean a thing. But I have drifted from psychotherapy to the question of awakening "work." So to another point.

<u>Guru</u>. You are not "denied" any methods of convincing yourself. But what "methods" are there? I never had any trouble recognizing the genuine—especially since you do not find it in a blue moon.

<u>Concepts</u>. "A new concept must either offer considerable data to indicate other concepts insufficient..." What is this vague sort of talk? Poppycock? <u>All</u> concepts are useless for our purpose. Talk English and give examples!

"<u>Loath to delineate that which you claim to know</u>." You still cling to the idea that there is something that can be explained—verbally of course. The general idea as far as words go has often been "explained," in the Oriental systems (avoiding "fancy" ideas such as those you mention), in Aldous Huxley's "Perennial Philosophy," in Brunton's "Wisdom of the Overself," and in all books that emphasize the one fact that we arise from (and return to) the one basis of the Universe.

"<u>What prevents suicide?</u>" The claims of life, friends, etc. "Survive" is our motto—while we can. Of course we "value" self, ego. We do not know what happens "after death." "Awakening" would give you a happier way of regarding this problem.

Friend,
Alfred

P.S. Skepticism, you may say, is helpful and unavoidable. Yes! But how many opportunities are lost that way for fear of a minor disappointment. And suppose you "skepticize" yourself right out of "awakening" work? <u>I know</u> that is very unfortunate, but I think <u>you</u> could go along without even an occasional twinge. I wish you could believe a friend and am sorry you can't. Oh well.

Dear Richard,

There <u>really is</u> a "way," you know, and you are on it—but at an <u>early stage</u>. Sorry you doubt my depth (!). So many of my students have recognized right away that I was 100 proof, 24 carat, the real McCoy! (Rare too!) I was surprised because there is no proof, but it wasn't a real surprise because I understand the phenomenon.

If you want to know how someone "feels" toward you, ask yourself how you feel about them. Action and reaction, says Sir Isaac Newton, are equal and opposite (and so far this law has held).

Feelings are funny things. So is friendship and love—defying reason—and since this matter we are dealing with is akin to both friendship and love ("one thing," anyway) it also defies reason—but not feeling.

Granted that one may be wrong once in a while, but after I have known a person a while then there is no such possibility. For example Brunton, Gurdjieff, Cagliostro, Nostradamus—all remarkable men—but I have only met one of them, Brunton, and that only twice, not enough to judge because I was then a seeker, in a highly emotional state, and a student myself. What about D.T. Suzuki, Sri Aurobindo? I met Suzuki twice. I am very suspicious here because they turned out such a big volume of words and theories. Zen masters do not do that!

Who would I regard as "awakened"? I think Krishnamurti, whom I have met, and the Maharshi, who has a down-to-earth common sense and is reasonably brief and to the point. (Plus thousands of unknowns!)

Maybe I should say that there is an

"intellectual" sort of "awakening" that produces a similar understanding and lasts through life (possible explanation why some men appear so wise), but which lacks simultaneous direct contact and ability to experiment with (!!) the Entity, which is the One.

"Mystical experience" is unconscious, or only partly conscious (and leaves ego untouched!). The need is to have this wonderful, but evasive and non-evidential thing, spread out for examination in the fully conscious mind—the one you use in your skeptical way (and believe me I am far more "skeptical" than you will ever be, being a mathematician and ex-public-accountant).

You keep falling over one and the same thing. You are looking in the South for the North star! To be specific, you raise questions as to life after death, reincarnation ("rebirth" is the Oriental word) and so forth. No answer to these has yet been furnished by experiment. That is the only way to get an "answer," if it is possible. (God tantalizes you with "ultimates.") However, when you become "awakened," your whole understanding of concepts, the self, time, space, perception, etc. is drastically overturned.

This, in turn, powerfully affects the consideration of your "questions." Obviously an "after-life," for example, implies that "time" goes on just as usual without your mind, or else that mind itself survives—and I doubt that!

Thus, questions are all disposed of, as mine have been, and in the following ways:

(a) Some are recognized as having no meaning in themselves and thus as "no-questions."

(b) Some are answered.

(c) Some are seen to be incapable of any answer (since they are things to be "accepted," like the One).

After awakening one feels this quietly happening for maybe a year after satori. "Maturing," we call it.

"Information?" You are ahead of yourself. For a .04 stamp you wish to peep at the hidden records of the Universe! Seriously, you must first get "awakening" to deal adequately with some of your "questions." Otherwise the answers would have been published long ago in the newspapers! Ever think of that? Words can be printed.

"Typical information." I note Brunton says Jesus came from another planet. This sort of "information" rings alarm bells in me at once, and involuntarily I say to myself, "Baloney. How does he know?"

"Reincarnation" is theosophy. In the East it is "rebirth," and that involves no real connection with you—only a continuation of "tendencies." *The Perennial Philosophy* contains innumerable quotations from genuinely awakened men. You refer to Huxley's writing style as "apologetic possibility." Why "apologetic"?

Am I an existentialist? I still don't know for sure what an existentialist is. What is it? Then I can say if I am one! Has "awakening" increased my knowledge of "life after death"? Certainly—but not as this "self."

Friend,
Alfred

P.S. At heart you are only a miracle-monger! The truth is not in that side of things—but nobody ever believes the warnings.

Dear Richard,

Query 1: "How can you be sure of me (Alfred) without having met me, when I said that even after meeting someone I wasn't sure of their attainment?"

Answer: Touché! Very reasonable, but who guaranteed the Buddha? This whole business reeks with paradox.

Considerations:

(1) If Krishnamurti offered to "work" with you, and to do so as a friend, then it would be foolish to refuse. He is a long way further on than you—and that I think is a reasonable inference (from lectures, books, acquaintance, etc.). My remark should not have been made. It turned on a very technical point only appreciable after experience.

(2) Do you ask a friend's bona-fides?

(3) Endless backchat! Unless you solve this dilemma somehow, "work" will never even begin! We are only "nagging" now.

(4) Act! Say "Yes" or "Goodbye," but reflect. To give an opinion is one thing, but to act is another. If I were "unawakened" and had the offer you had from some person claiming awakening, I would be careful not to lose him completely because if I was wrong I should have thrown away all that life has to offer, and if I was right I should have merely prevented some extra trouble for myself, writing, attending sessions or what not (where I could have acquired something anyway). (Pascal's wager all over again—but this time a clear dichotomy.) Time is now running out for you because we are at a definite impasse and writing is becoming futile—in fact, to be honest, it seems so now. Don't forget—I know "me," you don't. But I realize

this means nothing from your angle.

(5) Others "awakened." A lot of other people did not have your difficulty. They soon made up their minds. A few, however, refused abruptly and saved yak-yak.

Query 2: "A concept to be acceptable must explain more than its predecessors."

<u>Answer</u>: Experience—even sensory experience, as of a color or sound—is not describable or graspable by any kind of concept whatsoever. Experience is our goal.

Query 3: "Aquinas inferred that the finite mind can never perceive the infinite."

<u>Answer</u>: He may well have done so whilst writing all that nonsense (the "Summa Contra Gentiles," etc.), because that is the same state you are in—concepts. But six months before his death (and my authority is the Catholic Encyclopedia), he had such an experience that he said all his writings were "<u>chaff</u>" (actual word). Yet people still study the nonsense. The Catholic Encyclopedia's authority is a personal friend of Aquinas, and the episode is not controverted—except by the fact that idiots waste their lives on the "great" Summa, still. (Idiots study books and metaphysics. I was one.)

Query 4: "What do you think of Van der Leeuw's *Conquest of Illusion*?"

<u>Answer</u>: Ask Mac. It would be more to the point if you substituted Alfred for Van der Leeuw. I realize this is not a natural thing to do—but look at it (if you can!) from my angle. If you "work" with me then I am the "master," not all the authors of various books. Books will <u>not</u> produce awakening, however interesting and so forth.

Query 5: "The greatest difficulty I have with you is trying to put you in a category."

<u>Answer</u>: I have no category, and you might as well stop this foolish effort at being patronizing and the "great investigator." I am not threatening, believe me, but don't you agree we are getting nowhere? This must peter out, and that is always regrettable. We can however part pleasantly.

Friend,
Alfred

P.S. <u>Query 6</u>: (Sorry, I forgot this one, and it is a lulu.) "Let me ask you for the reasons for your interest in other people—is this some sort of law which must be followed, or do you expect further help for helping others?"

<u>Answer</u>: People are tethered to a pole like an animal. It is "self," ego, and it controls them. Thus they always look for an ego-motive, "What's in it for me?" etc., and this they regard as a <u>truism</u>! It reminds me of the science-fiction story where a man visited a planet where "utility" ruled. He observed their plain vases and cups and so on, and one day painted a pattern on one. Consternation! Whatever was the <u>utility</u> of this? (They could not understand any other reason for such an action, or any action.)

To be "outgoing," friendly for its own sake, is regarded on this third planet (Earth) as prime aberration, or fishy! However, if you want an ego-reason, let me say that I have been very well paid <u>in advance</u>, in a peculiar way.

But this is false as a reason because <u>nobody</u> takes money or its equivalent for this work unless in actual need—and then only as between friends who share all they have. (Don't be alarmed! I do not refer to all the fanciful organizations.)

P.P.S. On another plane, consider that we are disguised modes of the One Self-Consciousness, and although separated into so many of us, it strives to realize itself in each of us and to unite again. This is crudely stated I know, but not so far from the truth.

Psychologically, consider that as we descend into deeper and deeper depths of psychosis we tend to become more and more concentrated on self to the exclusion of others, even in the minutest details. Instead of being "open" we become "withdrawn." Thus sanity demands the attitude that so puzzles you.

Your motto is, "Stop giving 'me' facts, they confuse me." I refer to the "angelic Doctor" (Aquinas) query No. 3, also to query No. 2. As far as our "work," friendship is not a state you can <u>argue</u> yourself into. It happens or it doesn't, and there you are.

Dear Richard,

This is "me" speaking. Occasionally on the stage an actor will doff his "mask" and disguises and make-up and appear as himself. It is sometimes a very different personality, in fact usually. Thus, in this letter I am not speaking as "one of the few," or somebody who claims to "know" about what you call "essence" and I call the "One Self." I leave that to one side. I am just another human being in this letter, and I trust you will find me agreeable and courteous.

Unkindness. I think all of us humans should feel a deep sympathy for one another in this vale of tears. Thus any "caustic sarcasm" you may have found in any of my previous letters I deeply regret (from the point of view of this letter). Also the "vulgar choice of words" that you observed, and the possible "adolescent desire to shock." Also I regret any "nagging" you may have noticed. All such things are merely adding fresh disagreeableness to the ample supply that exists anyway.

Leaving with a dirty look. The few cases that I have had where a person withdrew were all characterized by more or less acerbity, and I think this is due to a misunderstanding. Let me illustrate.

The technique. A young girl student of Zen was walking along Sixth Avenue, New York, when a "drunk" decided to give her a scare. He shouted out something as loud as he could, "BOO!!" The girl smiled, as it reminded her of the Zen master. The drunk said, "Christ, she likes it!" You remember the character in the Mikado, who was unable to find anybody to contradict him? Everybody was too darn nice!

The person who is "awakened" understands that the only way to such an attainment is <u>against ego</u>. That means that the guru, or whatever you call him, has to be constantly throwing barbs, harpoons—being disagreeable, sarcastic, unreasonable, vulgar, adolescent, nagging, caustic and so forth. It is his job, as it is the job of the architect to design buildings.

<u>A thankless task</u>. Obviously it is a thankless task. He does not, I assure you, enjoy his role in life but, like a surgeon, he has a job to do. The results are beyond glory, and beyond all imagination, and any little temporary inconvenience is negligible—or should be.

<u>Kicking the surgeon</u>. But it is surprising how the slightest touch on our ego (and now that includes mine too, of course) makes us flare up, get resentful and so forth. We assume there is, as is usual in this world, no love behind the barbed insult, but <u>forget</u> that in the case of the guru (and my guru, too!), there is all the Love in the world! We mix up quarreling and nagging (so familiar in marital life and daily life) with the guru's technique.

<u>Find another one or drop the whole miserable business</u>. Now the poor guru doesn't want to keep up this stream of unreasonable invective, but it is the only way if results are to be achieved (ego must be desensitized). So if the pupil screeches loudly enough, the guru happily* gives up the whole horrible business and is only too glad* to get back on a mutually agreeable basis where friends (as the world understands that word) can interchange pleasant discussions about ultimate problems. (* Sadness, too, because another person has failed to see what was being aimed at, i.e. has "missed the mark.")

<u>Make up your mind</u>. If you regard the whole business as being nonsensical and leading nowhere

(and you are entitled to your point of view), then obviously the so-called guru is merely a disagreeable old bastard having a crude kind of fun with the poor student. From your point of view this is how I spend my life. Naturally from my point of view I think you have a caricature, because I can actually point to at least 70% of successes where the student was too grateful for any words and fully understood the means it was necessary to use to bring him or her to a realization.

<u>Battle against ole debbil ego</u>! Even psychotherapy—whose aim is more limited, and whose goal is not so far off—has to go contra-ego or contra-self to some extent. However, here the time is paid for, so it is possible by spreading out the annoyance over a long period to make the mental disturbance seem much less. We had farther to go and less time to do it in.

<u>Shadow boxing</u>. It is usual for an agreement to be reached so that although the guru and student are fencing, boxing or what have you, yet they agree that whatever injuries are received (not really very serious ones—only to the self-esteem!) they will remain friends and continue whatever happens. In this way Jacob wrestled with the Lord. Always their friendship is reaffirmed at the close of each letter.

<u>What I "wanted."</u> Naturally I wanted more than "a flow of correspondence" (especially when you refused to "argue," at times, and wrote only a couple of sentences).

(a) I did expect that you would appreciate my motives and the necessity of this unfortunate technique (monks have to be dragged in to face the Zen master sometimes—when they cannot answer their "koans"). If the fencing or boxing turns into a grudge-fight then the cooler head will call a halt, even apologize if necessary and politely avoid further occasions with the same person.

(b) I also expected that "friend" would gradually come to mean something, so that together we could examine what you call our "diversity in the field of metaphysics" and together make a reasonable decision about it. I must, however, protest against the word "metaphysics," as what happened to many other students was not an understanding of "metaphysics," but a conscious experience quite unlike anything else that happens all by itself when we cease to oppose the current of life.

<u>I did all you are doing now</u>. I will say that your present attitude is no different from that which I myself had to my own teacher or guru. (I wish I could avoid Indian terms as I am not concerned with Oriental metaphysics!) I was sullen, revengeful, spiteful, angry—more so in fact than yourself—even murderous, and we all have a touch of that in us.

It seems now that to be so moved by insults to my precious "super ego" is the most absurd thing in the world. But let a waiter say to you in a whisper, "Not that fork sir, use the other one," and you "burn" slowly (even if it is a practical joke). Self-esteem is awfully strong.

<u>Your nasty mind</u>. With a student like yourself it is <u>your interests solely</u> that are considered. What do I gain by the time I spend on these letters? The pleasure of being "sarcastic"? Hardly. That is Dead Sea fruit and a vain "pleasure." I have enough to trouble me in the natural course of life without seeking you out as a butt for mere rudeness! Besides, you don't have to take it, you know.

Thus, you can call me caustic and sarcastic (or far worse), but when you add "that I consider unnecessary," then I see that you are not clear as to what we are doing. If I were all sweetness and light, I somehow think it would not make much change in Richard! He can get that kind of glucose from a thousand easy sources (from the pulpit to the inspirational articles, books, pamphlets, etc.).

<u>You do not think that "awakening" means much</u>. I am not really a louse, but you have somehow to learn to handle these "harpoons" and not to regard it as a marital squabble. The real trouble, however, which makes our work so difficult is that you have no actual belief that there is any such experience (as I so often refer to as "awakening") available to human beings. Thus it all seems useless to you.

Your friend,
Alfred

April 29

Dear Richard,

Vitamin C: Would still feel inclined to "fill up" with vitamin C, say 4 of the 500 USP units tablets as indicated, and for a few days, until the "lemonade" color of the urine shows the system is "full." Only A and D seem to have side-effects, and those only in very abnormally high dosages, so the C can be taken safely — at least I have found it so, and a friend.

Reason! Do not preen yourself too much on being "logical." Much else enters into your "reasoning," which at times resembles the absurdities a poor subject of post-hypnotic suggestion has to emit! Suppose he is told he will take his pants down (in company) at a certain gesture — and it is given. He must say, "This may seem startling to you, but I feel the heat and although you may be shocked in appearance I know it is not real, and consequently I propose to remove my pants at this time. Let us all show our independence of conventional behavior..." and so forth.

Logic is all very well for a time, but at any real problem or obstacle emotionally affecting you, out comes the, "To hell with you, this is what I think, and I don't care what you say."

Actually, we "sweep things under the rug," you know. In the last century there was a mechanics-materialistic attitude, which seemed very solid and comforting, hard little particles, fixed laws. Even "chance" obeyed laws, and evolution "showed" how life, and later, consciousness evolved from, respectively, the mud and the monkey — at least it was assumed it was only a matter of time.

There was another "gap" at the vertebrates too.

Certainly no need for the God-hypothesis, or any form of teleology so hateful to research. So now space is finite but re-curves in the fourth dimension, two electrons are "wavicles," (wave-particles) and when they meet require six dimensions—also if one knows their velocity one cannot know their position, and vice versa. Anti-matter has arrived—negative "being"! The concept of consciousness or self has remained inscrutable, and "cause," "time," "infinity" we sweep under the rug with horror in our adolescence.

The vagueness, obscurity, abstraction, and so forth we accuse the "awakened" persons of are really our own baby. Nice baby! Such concepts are the opposite of clarity, reality, definiteness, and arise when we play at the edge of our playground. In other words, obfuscation is as natural to mind as clarity. But neither of these applies to the "awakened" person, who is aware of that which is beyond both reason and imagination. However, reason grows from experience, not experience from reason.

D.T. Suzuki told the Japanese Emperor on April 23, 1946 that, "We all, Buddhists as well as Christians, living as we do on the plane of the intellect, submit everything to intellectual test and domination, and reject as unworthy of consideration all that the intellect fails to understand."

The "scientific world" is pre-eminently the world of the intellect. However, this is a world of postulates and abstractions and concepts—remote from reality and constantly changing. Electricity, matter, mass, time, space, (curved space!), force, etc., are high-order abstractions derived from postulates, which lead to other postulates, and so back to experience (like pointer-readings, scintillations etc.). They are "sufficient" until proved wrong.

The "personal world" is quite different. This

consists of things for which there is <u>no</u> "reason," which cannot be described, which science cannot handle — such as colors (quite indescribable and nothing like the postulated "vibrations in the ether"), sounds (nothing like air compression and rarefication), emotions, feelings, affection, smell (nothing like the small particles thrown off by objects), touch (a diffused indescribable sense, if it is a sense), mind (psychology deals with everything <u>but</u> its subject-matter! e.g. behavior, reaction-times, etc., and never directly with the strange "nature" of the mental side of our organism).

There is a variable personal "time" that allows of no measurement, also. There is "consciousness," and scientists quietly assume this — until a blow on the head, or a sleeping pill removes the whole Universe in a split second!

These two worlds are assumed by Bertrand Russell to have a one-one correspondence. But further than that no man goeth. We do not even know if we see the same colors and hear the same sounds — as for example A♭ [A-flat] or C# [C-sharp].

"Reason," even if it were as cold as a calculating machine with no prejudices and errors punched on our memory-card (and there are plenty!), is only half the equipment of an integrated person. In Buddhism, the show-piece of the pimply-adolescent-intellectual, there is nevertheless both Mahaprajna, the Great Wisdom, and Mahakaruna, the Great Compassion — and these are not two but one and flow into one another.

"The highest reality" (I quote a Buddhist, Suzuki) "is not a mere abstraction. It is very much alive with sense and intelligence, and above all, with love purged of human infirmities and defilements." *

Sounds like "religion" doesn't it. Bambinos

with starched embroidery and laces, electric prayer wheels, consecrated wafers, bloody wine, priests, ministers, saints, devils, rabbis, men with clothes reversed and bits of their epidermis "sacredly" removed, black meteoric stones, rosaries, patient men with big red hearts on the outside, tambourines, drums, mighty Wurlitzers....

* But as it happens, it is true. (I refer to the * paragraph.) You cannot "pin down" an experience, and I cannot properly describe it. And if I could, it would not do the vital thing — produce it in you. That needs special techniques, continual squawks from you, and gray hairs for me.

I could not describe a blue flower to a blind man — he could feel its shape and texture, that is all. Would he feel annoyed at not "pinning me down"?

<u>Who is it then</u>? The "madball" is not me. I was educated as a mathematician at college, became a public accountant and worked on some of the biggest projects including UNRRA, became an executive, office manager, assistant treasurer — I was always very skeptical and hard-headed. My mind "contains" yours actually, although you could reach the same position, of course, and we were trying to do this. We are not unlike a man and quite a young child.

<u>St. Teresa et alia</u>. I am not driving at "mysticism," which is, as it happens, a valid <u>glimpse</u> of the One Self mentioned above. I am driving at this <u>in the conscious mind</u>, freely available for experiment and consideration. Not as a glimpse, but fully and for days and weeks. Not lost in semi-conscious ecstasy, but in calm appreciation of the greatest mystery life has to offer. Like seeing a joke suddenly, or leaping to a conclusion.

The truth does not permeate all religions except in such fantastic disguise that its own father wouldn't know it. Suppose truth is a rabbit. This rabbit is in a field — a large field. Round the field are very high walls — creeds and dogma! So — find your damn rabbit! And remember the rabbit knows your thoughts, and so as you resolve to go one way to catch it, it knows and evades you!

I do not refer to "ethics" but to attaining satori or awakening, "salvation." All religions are degenerated versions of the things the founder (such as Jesus, Buddha, Lao Tse, etc.) said — altered, added to, twisted and so forth, and completely useless because every time the founder opened his blessed mouth he put his blessed foot in it — and he knew it! (The Buddha said as much.) If then the true words of the founder are no damn good, what is the good of the decayed version called a religion?

If you preserved my letters and tried to help someone with them it would be no good. They are for you particularly, tailor-made, a "custom" job, and no good for others. That is why you have to shell out $25 for 40 minutes for an analyst. Reading Freud or Jung won't cure you! (Don't come back with a wearisome spiel about psychoanalysis. I only use it as an illustration of a relationship of one master to a pupil.) "No man can serve two masters." And no master can serve 1000 pupils — except one by one.

I was smarter than you. I saw where the shoe pinched. I saw that I had to do something that reason could not do because it could never understand itself! There was a bear in the cave and I had to get him out — and could only use tricks and persuasion until he decided to waddle out! I saw there was a dilemma. I saw that my egocentric position was in the way of a universal understanding. But how could I resolve not to decide, as "I" usually does? It was like lifting myself off the floor, or a knife cutting itself. So I considered the matter warily.

Rx: However, the prescription (what to do) is as old as the human race. Find a guru — and it wasn't easy. I tried Nikhilananda, a splendid man and a swami in the Ramakrishna mission on New York's East Side. Also Yoshikawa, a Buddhist priest at the temple not too far away from the previous Hindu, but this time a Japanese, of course. Also a Taoist, "in the succession," certainly "awakened," and well received in the temples of Zen in Japan. He was a European. None of these did the trick because I was, and am, far more obstinate and pig-headed even than you (and that's saying a lot).

One day while investigating a new psychotherapy I met a very self-possessed young lady, married, cheerful. I spoke to her, and then tried all my intellectual equipment (apart from skepticism you haven't exhibited much actual knowledge yet by the way) — the philosophers, scientists and so forth. Like you, I was stuffed to the gills with other people's ideas and as proud as a peacock. "We think," "we say," "we believe." Boy, was I a stinkeroo).

She handled these very easily. Compared to me she was deep water, deeper than my sonic apparatus could register. Could she be deeper than Vedanta, Shin-shu, Taoism, Zen? I was incredulous, but it has worked out. One day I may continue this — if you are good.

Learning, "digging," understanding. Anything I could "teach" you would be stupid because it could be printed, and indeed should have been printed long ago — for the whole world! That is ridiculous. No words will do the job if taken as a doctrine, theory or system.

I use words as a technique and consequently you must feel annoyed, frustrated, and all the rest of

116

it. Rejoice when that is so because it shows ego is getting a jab now and then. It cannot be pleasant. You know and I know that there are innumerable books on "our" subject — the One Self, the wisdom religion. It is no use to read them. So it would be useless to read me — as part of a system, doctrine, theory, or anything coherent.

Why do you persist in trying to compass by the intellect what is the one obvious thing that has never been so grasped? Our goal is beyond both thought and imagination. That does <u>not</u> mean impossible. The color blue — if you had not experienced it — is beyond both thought and imagination.

Even something "round the corner" is the same. There is no substitute for "experience." <u>This</u> "experience" <u>comes of itself</u> when you are at a certain stage. I always know where you are on the path, and at present you are near the beginning, of course.

You have probably not even read my last letter, and it was fairly lengthy. So is this. I have not tried to be obscure, just the reverse. But our subject is a technique for achieving something beyond reason, and that is quite a problem. If it wasn't you could get a paper book on it and 30 minutes would make you wise. But that is not how our Universe works. Jesus said the learned wouldn't understand him, simple people would. Well, that is true. But I am not simple nor are you — and I went through merry Hades and so apparently will you. Sorry bo.

Friend,
Al

P.S. Not too cantankerous, now am I?

Dear Richard,

No, it is very difficult to solve the cosmic problem oneself, because for the "self" to abandon — even for a fraction of a second, <u>which is all that is necessary</u> — its own proud assumption of being the ultimate decider is, as I have so often said, almost impossible. This is because to "decide" not to decide is a paradox, like lifting yourself up. Of course if you hold onto a horizontal bar you can lift yourself off the ground and in the same way you must use an awakened person to "help" (like the horizontal bar).

A person who will patiently "work" with you without complaining, without hope of reward or desire for it — for years if necessary — must have something, and it is rather over-skeptical to doubt it. No doubt there are a lot of goofy people who think they are a Jesus or God, but you can surely tell them pretty quickly and they are <u>not</u> the type to reason with you patiently for years.

If you will allow me to say so, your skepticism is beyond the ordinary allowance even for an "intellectual," and verges upon the ungracious and unkind. As a mathematician and former auditor my standards of proof are very, very high and exacting, but I do not "hold out" when a sufficient level of proof has been reached. In a bank audit or the audit of a commercial concern we were always watchful but did not fall into pathological doubt-fancies. When doubt ceases to be a servant and becomes your master, and you wonder if there is an octopus hiding behind the .04 stamp on my letter, then you are in a bad way.

Now unfortunately doubt in itself is not evil. But <u>allied to resistance</u> it can go against the flow of life, and I can usually tell by looking at a person or after a brief conversation, whether they are of this type—and so are dangerously vulnerable to tensions, lack of circulation and consequent bad troubles in the body. That is why such "constipated" and "withdrawn" obstinacy can crumple in a flood of tears at a religious healing meeting—and actually produce results! (Whether the religion taught is nonsense or fact is not the point. It is the softening of attitude that is so vital. We try to be so rock-ribbed, we poor mortals!)

Fortunately, even though life may get rough "all will be well, very well." I cannot logically prove this, but it is a fact (if you will let your friend make a mere assertion of what is true by his own experience), and it is a fact according to a lot of others too, that there is a Something that seeks us—individually and personally—with a humility and open simplicity we lack. The poem, "The Hound of Heaven," by Francis Thompson illustrates this. ("I fled Him, down the nights and down the days...")

It does not matter when you encounter such a person as myself, except that if you do not feel well, it is much harder for you to "work." In your case, not being a medical man, I do not know what thing will help one of your troubles and harm another perhaps. My own teacher, when her mother had bad bronchitis (had to have injections), gave her some high potency C-vitamin tablets and told her to eat them freely! (A 500 mg tablet of vitamin C is equivalent perhaps to a quart of orange juice.)

For a condition like that I would get the 100 tablets of 500 mg vitamin C from Hudson for $1.35, or if the acid was not desired, then get the Plus Formula 279, vitamin C powder, 50 grams—$1.95, "soluble in cold liquid, acid-free" from Plus Products. Maybe you would ask your doctor to see if it would do harm. If not, try it, because I wouldn't be stopped merely by the fact that the use of massive doses of C to reduce infections is experimental. Has been since 1948. When will they "know"? (Of the 100 tablets or the 50 grams of powder, I would use in my own case half during one week, then rest a week, then use the other half. This works out to about 7 tablets a day or 3500 mg a day, or about 3 1/2 grams a day.)

Also, I feel that yogurt would possibly be helpful, and containers of this are easily available at .19 and .25, which will last two times at least. Also, Plus Products has a fine Torula Yeast, which provides a good balance of the B vitamins, an almost complete protein (it is 50% protein anyway), and lots of minerals). I do not want to divert your mind, however, from the suggestions on page 2 which you could check. Nor do I know if you are dieting or how.

"Awakening" is perhaps a sad knowledge—like growing up! But I asked my teacher if she would "go back" and she said "No!" Now I myself can answer my own question! My answer is, "I would not think of it! No!" I remember in New York getting a telephone installed for her and her husband. I felt, "This is the end! Tomorrow there will be thousands of people lining the street and sitting on the sidewalk and steps—all waiting to see her and get enlightenment."

Surprise! There was not even one. Only me and a few private students of hers. Nor are there more than a handful who write to me now. Yet this is worth more than all the wealth of the world because the wealth of the world will not buy it.

When I was young I day-dreamed of course, and thought I would like to be not famous but wise! The "power behind the throne," another Richelieu!—

120

knowing more than professors, scientists, religious leaders, philosophers, everybody! Now I do know more than most and the pride is no longer there. That is dust and ashes, burnt out. There is much sympathy left and I do what I can, and sometimes I get beautiful letters full of gratitude—rarely from "famous" people, although I know two or three authors, and lawyers, a minister or two, housewives, psychotherapists, night-watchmen, bum, Buddhists, Jews, Christians, agnostics. But none in the topmost ranks, like Jung and so forth.   Jesus said they were too smart for their own good. I was too. What an insufferable, snooty, sneery, smart-aleck I was. (Hope I have improved at least a little!) I knew it all. My mind was free from prejudice, open, capable of judging—in a pig's eye! A good thing we don't know our own motives and weaknesses.

Our intellect is based on a miscellaneous grab-bag of assorted memory-junk and prejudices arrived at largely by accident (what we read, heard, saw). We are not even properly programmed for our job like an IBM machine!

Yet these chance memories give the flavor to our "I" that we call "personality." (We "remember" things we do not properly understand or respond to, apart from certain useful facts.) Thus the much-vaunted "I" is a collection of half-understood perceptions! And this bemused captain controls the vessel we call our "body." He is only "conscious" a few minutes at a time during the day! Rulers of the earth! Voyagers to the stars! (with a trail of empty beer-cans and, mentally, a cargo of aberrations, for Alpha-Centauri!)

I wish we were kinder to the animals. I wish we were kinder to one another. There is nobody on earth, even Khrushchev, who will not feel one day his or her utter loneliness, utter insulation from any other human being. To avoid knowing this we engage in commerce (must work to eat you say? Yes, but I have known millionaires go on working!) and fill our time with distractions.

The "work" I do helps toward breaking down this separation we human-beings feel. It is not necessary. It is only the impulse to defend ourselves—we are terribly afraid of "coming out" just as ourselves and being stepped on!

This is a false fear. A lot of people, some professional speakers and entertainers, are quite "open" (Will Rogers), and I do not mean backslappers.

This "I" of ours has a better side of course. Its basis—apart from memories—is the strange "self" conception. This is a direct reflection of the One Self, and it is this we can see in one another.

Friend,
Alfred

Volume VI　♦　Number 3

The Penny That Blots Out the Sun

By ALFRED R. PULYAN

IT WAS in the little western town of Berree. I faced the committee. Mr. Aleph Norte, the chairman, looked at me severely. "You know our principles," he said. "Seek and ye shall seek. Knock and we hope nothing happens."

"I do," I replied. I knew that Mr. Norte had had a very trying month, On his arrival at Berree, he had made no secret that he was and always had been a gold-seeker. There was an avalanche. Many sought to sell him their mines; many, however, offered them to him freely. It was necessary to impose stringent conditions. The gold must be officially assayed at 100 percent, it must be on the surface, it must be near at hand. Even then a committee was necessary to strain out all the applicants.

"I notice in your offer," said Mr. Norte, "that the gold is pure and beautiful and lies on the surface ready for the taking. However, you state that it lies on a road half-a-mile to the north. Now, all of us here know for a certainty that there cannot be only one way. We are here to investigate every way and are willing to spend our money and time in continual seeking. We are, therefore, sorry to refuse your offer, the more so as we love people."

This was not the first time I had made a mistake. Without thinking, I blurted out the truth. *"Actually, the gold lies in a half-mile circle. It is all around you. You cannot fail to find it--if, of course, you wish."*

There was a tense and terrible silence. Then, they came towards me.

How did I escape? I did not. The place was a shambles. There were bits of me all over the place, and so I feel free to tell you what the committee would not listen to-- the actual way in which a student is brought to "awakening", always has been and, as you will easily see for yourself, always will be-- until our species develops a new faculty or somebody bursts this ball.

Your first problem is a teacher, "opener", master, or whatever you like to call him (or her). Let us take a specific example: Subud. This rests on perfectly valid experiences of Muhammad Subuh of Java; in particular on one that happened on the night of June 21-22, 1933.

As has happened many times in history (with the "Buddha" Gautama as an example), a "movement" started from this one man and has become world-wide. Groups of people are meeting everywhere under the guidance of so-called "helpers", and from these, people who are suitable will proceed to centers for direct work.

Awakened and "matured" persons will be needed to do this work. All must derive from Pak (Father) Subuh himself. Awakening may take anything from 30 minutes to 10 years or more, and usually takes several years under favorable conditions. Further, this awakening varies and many do not have either the desire or capacity to awaken others, and rest content with their attainment, spreading what light they can to those around them.

Groups are everywhere in the world. What will happen to this flood of people? Clearly, Subud will develop into a sort of religion and will offer much consolation to those content with the meetings and unable or unwilling to proceed further. That is, in fact, what religions are. There are tens of thousands of awakened people in the U. S., but if these "work", they work alone, and converts to Subud, who trust Pak Subuh, do not trust them.

On the other hand, there is a Zen Master in this country (or soon should be) and those working with him would not be much inclined to switch to Subud.

It seems that there are as many brands of awakening as of coffee, and that it is the well-advertised ones that attract people. They do not differ much actually in method and not at all in result since, as you will see, their problem is the same.

How can we sum this up? Clearly, Zen is a sure way because a succession of enlightened Masters is rigidly maintained, but it is apt to be a very lengthy process. It is also a tough one, but so it has to be in any system. Even in Subud there is an "O" group kept separate because of their violent reactions.

Many are afraid of the whole business because they suspect or rationalize that it is autosuggestion. I know very well, for what it is worth to you, that you are more free than before, not less free. Moreover, if it is time for you to start this process, you will not have much to say about it anyway. We have a saying that when the student is ready the master appears. It does seem to work that way.

The harvest, however, is plentiful but the laborers are few.

Let me consider the problem of working with a person like you, the reader. Normally, if you wish to know something you get a book on the subject or attend lectures or ask a friend. If the subject is not too complicated, you anticipate that, by directing your mind and memory to it, you will see "what it is all about" and finish up with a good working knowledge of the subject. If the subject is very important, your mind becomes as alert as a tiger. It is the way of our minds (and many of the new calculating machines) to dichotomize, to tear things in half. Unfortunately, this process does not work with any "ultimate" problem and only results in the mind breeding more and more thoughts about it unendingly--like grasshoppers.

It so happens that the peculiar origin of you and the universe is concealed in a place that the mind cannot reach. Some persons will call this "God", but this word will mislead you and it is better to find out what this is yourself and then call it what you like.

Most persons think of themselves as twofold. There is "my" consciousness, "my" mind, "my" self on the one hand-- and on the other, "my" body. This is all of me. There is a decided split between these two sides of me.

The Penny That Blots Out the Sun

Alfred R. Pulyan

Even with a Teacher, the Student Sets Up Many Dodges to Protect His "My" Consciousness from the Triumphant Experience of Full Awakening

It was in the little western town of Berree. I faced the committee. Mr. Aleph Norte, the chairman, looked at me severely. "You know our principles," he said. "Seek and ye shall seek. Knock and we hope nothing happens."

"I do," I replied. I knew that Mr. Norte had had a very trying month. On his arrival at Berree, he had made no secret that he was and always had been a gold-seeker. There was an avalanche. Many sought to sell him their mines; many, however, offered them to him freely. It was necessary to impose stringent conditions. The gold must be officially assayed at 100 percent, it must be on the surface, it must be near at hand. Even then a committee was necessary to strain out all the applicants.

"I notice in your offer," said Mr. Norte, "that the gold is pure and beautiful and lies on the surface ready for the taking. However, you state that it lies on a road half-a-mile to the north. Now, all of us here know for a certainty that there cannot be only one way. We are here to investigate every way and are willing to spend our money and time in continual seeking. We are, therefore, sorry to refuse your offer, the more so as we love people."

This was not the first time I had made a

mistake. Without thinking, I blurted out the truth. *"Actually, the gold lies in a half-mile circle. It is all around you. You cannot fail to find it — if, of course, you wish."*

There was a tense and terrible silence. Then, they came towards me.

How did I escape? I did not. The place was a shambles. There were bits of me all over the place, and so I feel free to tell you what the committee would not listen to — the actual way in which a student is brought to "awakening," always has been and, as you will easily see for yourself, always will be — until our species develops a new faculty or somebody bursts this ball.

Your first problem is a teacher, "opener," master, or whatever you like to call him (or her). Let us take a specific example: Subud. This rests on perfectly valid experiences of Muhammad Subuh of Java; in particular on one that happened on the night of June 21-22, 1933.

As has happened many times in history (with the "Buddha" Gautama as an example), a "movement" started from this one man and has become world-wide. Groups of people are meeting everywhere under the guidance of so-called "helpers," and from these, people who are suitable will proceed to centers for direct work.

Awakened and "matured" persons will be needed to do this work. All must derive from Pak (Father) Subuh himself. Awakening may take anything from 30 minutes to 10 years or more, and usually takes several years under favorable conditions. Further, this awakening varies and many do not have either the desire or capacity to awaken others, and rest content with their attainment, spreading what light they can to those around them.

Groups are everywhere in the world. What

will happen to this flood of people? Clearly, Subud will develop into a sort of religion and will offer much consolation to those content with the meetings and unable or unwilling to proceed further. That is, in fact, what religions are. There are tens of thousands of awakened people in the U.S., but if these "work," they work alone, and converts to Subud, who trust Pak Subuh, do not trust them.

On the other hand, there is a Zen Master in this country (or soon should be) and those working with him would not be much inclined to switch to Subud.

It seems that there are as many brands of awakening as of coffee, and that it is the well-advertised ones that attract people. They do not differ much actually in method and not at all in result since, as you will see, their problem is the same.

How can we sum this up? Clearly, Zen is a sure way because a succession of enlightened Masters is rigidly maintained, but it is apt to be a very lengthy process. It is also a tough one, but so it has to be in any system. Even in Subud there is an "0" group kept separate because of their violent reactions.

Many are afraid of the whole business because they suspect or rationalize that it is autosuggestion. I know very well, for what it is worth to you, that you are more free than before, not less free. Moreover, if it is time for you to start this process, you will not have much to say about it anyway. We have a saying that when the student is ready the master appears. It does seem to work that way.

The harvest, however, is plentiful but the laborers are few.

Let me consider the problem of working with a person like you, the reader. Normally, if you wish to know something you get a book on the subject or attend lectures or ask a friend. If the subject is not too complicated, you anticipate that, by directing your mind and memory to it, you will see "what, it is all about" and finish up with a good working knowledge of the subject. If the subject is very important, your mind becomes as alert as a tiger. It is the way of our minds (and many of the new calculating machines) to dichotomize, to tear things in half. Unfortunately, this process does not work with any "ultimate" problem and only results in the mind breeding more and more thoughts about it unendingly — like grasshoppers.

It so happens that the peculiar origin of you and the universe is concealed in a place that the mind cannot reach. Some persons will call this "God," but this word will mislead you and it is better to find out what this is yourself and then call it what you like.

Most persons think of themselves as twofold. There is "my" consciousness, "my" mind, "my" self on the one hand — and on the other, "my" body. This is all of me. There is a decided split between these two sides of me.

However, the fact is all of these are one; that is, my mind and my body are one — one organism, not two.

But this does not exhaust the situation. There is a pure Consciousness — Consciousness that knows itself. "I am that I am." This is unexpected and I did not believe when I first heard this that there could be two kinds of Consciousness. I only knew the one I was naturally familiar with, the "I am as I am."

The way it works is this. This pure Consciousness shines on the mind-and-body organism; it is the "light that lighteth every man that cometh into this world." When it does this it suffers a change. My mind accepts it only as "my consciousness" — a limited consciousness — and, since Its essence is Self-Consciousness, "I" experience It in a

128

similar way as a self, in fact "myself," or ego. I say I am "conscious of myself," but this is a smaller self, not the Universal One, merely what I call "me," one of my many "me's."

It may be said that the pure Consciousness is concealed in "my" consciousness as a penny may hide the sun. A ray of this may suddenly dazzle us in so-called "mystical experiences," of which most persons have had a touch, but in awakening (or satori or metanoia) we see the pure Consciousness shining serenely in its own light. It is a triumphant experience since "what has to be done" has been done, but it is also profoundly humbling as our little self sees itself as a usurper, a thief borrowing its selfhood from the Universal Self.

A student wrote me: "Consciousness sees itself. It is impossible yet it happens."

So much for theory. The practical job of awakening someone consists in part of showing him or her by various devices that all mental attempts to reach the pure Consciousness are in vain. It lies back of our mind and back of our consciousness. Any thought we have about it is impartially irradiated by it. For example, we think "this is unproved idiocy" and the pure Consciousness lights it up in its usual benevolent way so that it becomes "I am aware that I think this is unproved idiocy."

Obviously, this is a peculiar situation. This Consciousness is at all times ready to make us "aware" of what we are thinking or perceiving, but that does not mean that we become aware of That which is Itself giving us this peculiar faculty of being aware of ourselves and our processes. Thus we get no clue as to whether our thought was a correct one or not; only that we know we have such a thought.

No wonder It is hidden and confusing. The

problem is to reach Consciousness as it is in itself and not as reflecting some thought or perception of ours that is in it at the time.

We require empty Consciousness so to say. Some try, like the Yogis or some of them, to attain it by emptying the mind by "meditation," but it is not the mind we have to empty. The real obstacle, of course, is the "my" concept, the self or ego. This is my Enemy in this work. How can we get from "my" consciousness to "the" Consciousness?

Naturally, as long as "we" decide or "we" try to do this, we are regarding ourselves as ultimate and reinforcing the bonds of delusion. All we do is rotate our own ideas like a squirrel in a cage. It would seem, therefore, an impossible task like lifting ourselves up by our own bootstraps.

However, the simple fact is that it happens all the time. There is help from the side of the Consciousness itself (theologians call this "Grace") which is not resting idly but presses to "come out" in us. There are intimations of what this pure Consciousness is like in music and the arts, in nature, and the highest aspirations we have.

The teacher (I wish I had a better word) takes advantage of these. Further, he stays "open" with the student, and the student, by mere love and friendship, receives what in Zen is called "transmission" and in Subud "contact." It is inevitable that the student should carefully observe every word and action of the teacher (because at first he doubts him) and in time the awakening of the teacher is felt definitely by the student, although not verbally definable.

In Zen, so-called "koans" are used to throw the mind out of the reasoning rut (in these days of paper books, I assume the reader knows what koans are) and sudden shocks are contrived to shake out the obstinate ego. The teacher uses similar things.

For months, the student tries every possible argument. Over and over, he will bring up. for example, the "problem of evil," the question of life after death, of reincarnation, of some religion or other he may have been taught in childhood, of science, of his own desperation at ever getting anywhere, of how one can tell if the realization, if it comes, is any more "real" than anything else, if it is merely another trick of the versatile mind or subconscious, whether we are just bubbles — anything and everything.

It is nothing new to-the teacher. He could write the script himself. (In fact, I have partly done so here.) However, he remains steady; he knows what has to be done, he knows where the student is and in time be sees hopeful signs.

The student is disturbed. He has come to the end of his "tricks" (actually desperate attempts to preserve the ego as boss, when it is only a competent executive officer) and the teacher will not "buy" any of such tricks.

The student is not a fool. He knows all the time what he is doing and that one day he must surrender in utter helplessness. Meanwhile, he retains a second line of defense, a "secondary" judgment which does not yield whatever he may say openly. One day this too lapses, even if only for a moment.

Then something happens. The student is surprised to notice, for example, that his perceptions are sharper, everything seems brighter. Next morning he awakens to a situation which puzzles him for a moment. Something is missing. What can it be?

He soon finds out. For a time he enjoys the extraordinary experience of being a limited ego with an unlimited Consciousness. He is free to use it and to test it. He finds It will show him the basis behind material things, the many in the One, a clear but absolutely new and indescribable thing; or it makes clear once and for all, the whole process of the ego or self in himself and others and in relationship. For a salesman or lawyer, this is indeed a bonanza, but there is a price to pay—he is not likely to use this new wisdom for wrong.

He now knows intimately—more intimately than we can know anything or anybody—the Basis of our universe and us and is perforce henceforward a "channel" and a servant of "That." It is a strange feeling for a proud man.

The job is not done. There ensues a long maturing process. Confused areas of thought, mental blockages, must yield one by one. He has the means to do this, but uses it naturally. One day the last weed is gone from his garden and he is surprised to find he has no further questions.

Do not think that this is all a mental exercise. It involves the whole organism, body and mind. It is a criticism of Zen that this feature is not stressed at all. In Subud, remarkable cures have occurred and readers may remember another great man who went about doing good—he could not avoid it. People will not flock for enlightenment, but will try anything to cure a so-called chronic condition.

What happens to the student after his experience has matured? It becomes the most natural thing in the world. He may say, like Gautama, that he has done nothing at all. It is true that he has "done" nothing, but he does know by actual experience what our human situation really is.

There is much difference between experience and words. You are welcome to laugh at my words. I do not think you would laugh at the experience.

Do not find this article too disturbing. You will

find that God is both "open" and loving—devastatingly, almost unbearably, so.

If you should find that the thought of God is constantly in your mind, do not try to remove it; it can be very unsettling. Welcome it and in time it will seem supremely right.

www.ingramcontent.com/pod-product-compliance
Lightning Source LLC
Chambersburg PA
CBHW061136160726
48006CB00038B/2120